*The*REVIVAL JOURNEY

JOHN R. VAN GELDEREN

FOREWORD BY RICK FLANDERS

REVIVALFOCUS

PRESS

THE REVIVAL JOURNEY

© 2010 John R. Van Gelderen

Published by Revival Focus Press, Germantown, WI.
www.RevivalFocus.com

Scripture quotations are taken from the King James Version of the Bible.

Graphic Design: www.FundamentalMedia.org

ISBN 978-0990669319

Printed in the United States of America

Contents

FOREWORD

Many Christians and Christian congregations today are ripening for revival. This book by John R. Van Gelderen is going to help them find their way down the road that leads to revival. The ripening I see is the result of a sense of emptiness, both on the right and on the left of evangelicalism. On the left, many feel empty because they are seeing through the superficial gloss of the entertainment model of worship, as well as the shallowness of marketing-oriented church growth. On the right, many feel empty after years of "doing church" based on rules rather than reality. The fact is that the evangelistic motives of some who lead the church-growth movement are not wrong, though some of their methods are, and the high standards maintained in the conservative churches are not wrong and should not be thrown away. The emptiness is caused by what is missing in many churches, both on the left and on the right: the manifest presence of Jesus Christ. His real presence (experienced through the ministry of His Spirit), both in the meetings of the church and in the lives of the members, is what gives them life. Services are not livened up by carnal, sensual music. According to the Bible, carnality has a deadening effect. "To be carnally minded is death, but to be spiritually minded is life and peace," says Romans 8:6. Only the Spirit of Life brings life, and the life He brings is Jesus Himself (John 1:4; 14:6). By definition, revival is the restoring of life to Christians and churches. This book is about revival, the divine work that is so needed in this time of emptiness among God's people.

Without question, there is a journey in and toward revival. Anyone who has known the impact of genuine, God-given revival realizes this fact. Their personal testimonies reveal it. The reality that most believers in Christ know little of the abundant life He came for them to experience explains why we must travel down a road to get to it. In this book, an evangelist well acquainted with that road, both from Scripture and from experience, helps us understand it and travel it. Brother Van Gelderen's thoughts in this regard are being published at the right time and with the blessing of God will do much good in forwarding the work that the Lord is doing in the world. Read these pages carefully; and with the thirst of a seeker, let the truth guide you to the place of victory and power.

> *"Humble yourselves in the sight of the Lord,*
> *and he shall lift you up."*
> *—James 4:10*

Rick Flanders

PREFACE

Revival is still God's answer!

The Revival Journey maps out the discernable phases of revival revealed in Scripture and illustrated by history. As such, it may serve as a practical manual for those seeking to exercise faith for revival. Yet at the same time, it may serve as a theological manual for those seeking to understand the theology of revival.

A reverse order of the phases of revival is incorporated in the first five chapters. Through this unusual approach, it is hoped that the later phases of the revival journey, which will be read first, will produce desire for the reader to take seriously the early phases of the revival journey, which will be read last, and inspire him to start the journey. Then a sixth chapter addresses key related concepts. Although of necessity personal revival is addressed throughout the work, the emphasis of this book is corporate revival.

It is my prayer that through the Word and the Spirit, as well as through remembering the wonderful works of God in history, that The Revival Journey will be a faith-builder to all who read it with an open heart, causing them to embark or be furthered on their own revival journey.

John R. Van Gelderen
May 2009
Ann Arbor, Michigan

The REVIVAL
JOURNEY

Chapter One

LIFE AGAIN!

*I*t's almost like getting saved again!" Often individuals declare this testimony when they experience revival. But what does this mean? What is revival?

Misconceptions of revival are many and varied. For example, some misconstrue counterfeit revival for genuine revival. At the turn of the century, there was a phenomenon known as the "laughing revival." Reports said that on occasion even when the preacher preached on the subject of hell, the crowd would break out laughing—but hell is not a laughing matter. This reveals a counterfeit revival. Yet in order to have a counterfeit of something, there must first of all be something real. Sometimes sincere people seek God's face, and God begins to bless in real revival. But because of a lack of grounding in truth, these sincere people can easily fall prey to satanic counterfeits. When counterfeits are embraced, the Holy Spirit is grieved away. Often the revival is then discredited because of the "strange fire" that may follow.

Another major misconception is confusing *revival* with a "meeting." Sometimes when church folk invite others to a special meeting that is taking place in their church, they will say to the person they are visiting, "We're having revival this week." What they mean is "We're having a meeting this week." Obviously, in these kinds of meetings people ought to be seeking God for revival. For it is certainly possible to have revival in a meeting. Yet just as obviously, not every meeting is on the level of real revival. A church sign once read "One Day Revival" and gave the date. Apparently what they meant was that they were planning a special day. Once in a six-day meeting that began on Sunday and was scheduled to end on Friday, the pastor stood up on Thursday evening and announced, "Now, the revival ends on Friday night!" These examples reveal how the word *revival* is being used synonymously with the word *meeting*. However, this usage softens and confuses the real understanding of true revival.

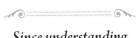

Since understanding the biblical concept of revival is vital to being able to properly seek God for revival, believers must accurately understand revival.

While it is fair and good to use the terminology "a revival meeting," which indicates a meeting for the purpose of seeking revival, it is unwise to use the word *revival* interchangeably with the word *meeting*.

In Psalm 85:6, the psalmist prays, "Wilt thou not revive us again: that thy people may rejoice in thee?" But what does it mean for God to "revive" His people? What is revival? How would one know if revival occurred? Since understanding the biblical concept of revival is vital to being able to properly seek God for revival, believers must accurately understand revival. By investigating the biblical words and concepts of revival, three defining issues may be distinguished regarding revival.

THE DEFINING ESSENCE OF REVIVAL IS A RESTORATION TO SPIRITUAL LIFE

The defining *essence* of revival refers to that which is *essential* regarding revival. The essence of revival refers to what revival *is*—not what revival *does*. For example, some say that if revival is not "coast-to-coast" it is not real revival. Or if revival does not shut down the bars in a community and so forth, it is not real revival. But what if one's country does not have two coasts, or what if there were no bars in a given community? While anyone with a heart for revival would desire results of this kind, this type of thinking confuses the extent of revival and/or the difference between what revival *does* and what revival *is*. What revival *does* will vary based on the needs in a given situation. Therefore these incidents are *incidental* in that they will vary from revival to revival. This does not mean these incidents are unimportant and cannot be reveled in as the wonderful works of God. It simply means they are not essential to every revival. What revival *is* will always be the same and therefore refers to that which is *essential* because it is the core issue of every revival. Simply put, there is a difference between what revival *may do* in a given scenario versus what revival *is* in every scenario.

Therefore in defining revival, one must clarify between what revival *is* rather than what revival *does*. Often definitions of revival are actually descriptions of revival. But descriptions are not the same as definitions. Revival definitions must focus on what revival *is*. Revival descriptions may focus on what revival *does*. Confusing the two issues may hinder revival. For example, in defining salvation, if what salvation *does* is confused with what salvation *is*, one may easily embrace a "struggle theology" or a flesh-dependent, works-perspective in an effort to be saved. Likewise in revival, if what revival *does* is confused with what revival *is*, one may easily embrace a "struggle theology" or a flesh-dependent, works-perspective in an effort to be revived. Revival definitions must therefore focus on what revival *is*.

The word *revive* in Psalm 85:6 translates from the Hebrew word *chayah*. The basic usage of the word in the Old Testament is "to live or have life" with a wide range of applications including physical life, emotional vitality, spiritual life, and so forth. But at times the word is used as a verb form meaning "to restore to life."[1] This sense can also include a variety of nuances, but for the purpose of this study the focus will be on the concepts of physical revival (for the sake of analogy) and spiritual revival.

Physically, the word is used in I Kings 17:17–24. The widow's son had died. Elijah came and prayed for the boy. Then the Scripture says, "and he *revived*" (v. 22). Clearly, the son of the widow was restored to physical life.

Spiritually, the word *chayah* is used in Psalm 85:6 with the sense of being restored to spiritual life. It is used in this sense eleven times in Psalm 119, translated in the KJV as "quicken" or "quickened" (Psalm 119:25, 37, 40, 50, 88, 93, 107, 149, 154, 156, 159). Nine of these occurrences are prayers for revival (all but v. 50 and v. 93) as well as Psalm 80:18; 85:6; 143:11; and the more familiar prayer of Habakkuk 3:2, "O Lord, revive Thy work." Of the thirteen prayers incorporating *chayah*, ten are prayers for personal revival (Ps. 119: 25, 37, 40, 88, 107, 149, 154, 156, 159; 143:11), and three are prayers for corporate revival (Ps. 80:18; 85:6; Hab. 3:2). The word is also used in the spiritual sense in contexts other than prayer. Although some passages might be debatable as to whether or not the spiritual sense of revival is the specific nuance used, clear passages include Psalm 138:7 (cf. v. 6); Hosea 6:2; 14:7, and the classic Isaiah 57:15, "to revive the spirit of the humble, and to revive the heart of the contrite ones."

The Hebrew *chadash* means "to renew" and is used in the sense of spiritual revival in Psalm 51:10 and Lamentations 5:21. However, contextually the emphasis is more on what revival

While it is legitimate to apply this parable to the lost, it is significant to note that the son is a son and the father is the father.

does than on what revival *is*. Also there are other Hebrew words that refer to the other phases leading up to revival. One example is the word *shub*, meaning "to turn back or return" and referring to the brokenness or repentance that leads to revival. But when it comes to revival itself, the Hebrew word *chayah* is the primary word, meaning, as already noted in the spiritual sense, "to restore to spiritual life."

The Greek counterpart to the Hebrew *chayah* is *anazao*. The word *anazao* is a compound word combining *ana*, indicating the idea of "again," with the verb *zao*, meaning "to live."

Therefore the complete thought is "to live again,"[2] or "come to life again."[3] In the physical sense, the word is used of Jesus Christ in Romans 14:9, which states that "Christ both died, and rose, and *revived.*" In the spiritual sense, the word occurs twice in the parable of the prodigal son. While it is legitimate to apply this parable to the lost, it is significant to note that the son is a *son* and the father is the *father.* The interpretation appears to be dealing with a prodigal son, in the sense of a child of God who is estranged from his Heavenly Father, being revived. Yet this is like one who is "lost" being "found" (Luke 15:24b, 32b). In the parable after the wayward son returned to his father, the father said, "For this my son was dead, and is *alive again*" (Luke 15:24a; cf. v. 32a). Obviously, the son was not dead physically. Therefore the father is speaking of a spiritual deadness and a restoration to spiritual life. *Alive again* is the translation of *anazao* and beautifully portrays the concept of revival. Revival is life again!

The New Testament uses several other "*ana* words" that are closely related to *anazao*: *anakainizo* (Heb. 6:6), *anakainoo* (II Cor. 4:16; Col. 3:10), *anakainosis* (Rom. 12:2), and *ananeoo* (Eph. 4: 23). All mean "to renew" or "renewal." In some contexts the nuance is quite close to *anazao*. In other contexts the nuance varies. However, when focusing on what revival *is, anazao* is the key word because it focuses on restoration to *life* as does the Hebrew *chayah*.

It may be wondered why there are not more usages of *anazao* in a spiritual sense in the New Testament. The answer is quite simple. The New Testament emphasis is not that you receive life, backslide, and then get revived. The New Testament emphasis is that you receive life and then live in that abundant life. Jesus said, "I am come that they might have life, and that they might have it more abundantly" (John 10:10). The New Testament focus is that the life of Christ be manifested in the believer as the standard and norm. Also the narrative section of the New Testament, which is the book of Acts, covers only about forty years. This brief span of time cannot compare to the hundreds of years recorded in the Old Testament, which allowed for historical cycles to be included. Yet Acts reveals that it is possible to experience a generation of revival.

Having surveyed the Hebrew and Greek words for *revive*, one finds that the English word conveys the same thought of restoration to life. When Noah Webster published the first edition of the *American Dictionary of the English Language*, the year was 1828. This was during the Second Great Awakening, following one of the major peaks of the revival that occurred in the early 1820s. Also, Webster was a personal friend of Asahel Nettleton, who was one of the evangelists greatly used of God in New England during the Second Great Awakening. This timing and background is important because when Webster produced his dictionary, he simply wrote definitions to words based on their usage in America. Providentially, he penned definitions for revival terminology at a time when revival was actually taking place all around him and had been for a quarter of a century. This is a significant fact.

As would be expected, Webster provided many nuances for the term *revival*. The purpose of this study focuses on the nuances of physical and spiritual revival. Concerning the physical concept of the word *revive*, Webster gives the definition as "to return to life; to recover life"; then he

immediately provides an illustration from Scripture found in
I Kings 17:22: "And the Lord heard the voice of Elijah; and
the soul of the child came into him again, and he revived."[4]
Regarding the spiritual concept of *revive*, Webster gives the
definition as "to bring again to life; to reanimate"; then he
provides an illustration from Psalm 85:6: "Wilt thou not revive
us again: that thy people may rejoice in thee?"[5] His definition
for the participle *reviving* is "bringing to life again."[6]

Revival [*re* (again) / *vive* (live or
life)] is clearly *life again*. Physically,
revival is a restoration to physical
life. Therefore, spiritually, revival
is a restoration to spiritual life.
But what life is that? The answer
may be found in the words of John
3:16. When someone believes
on Jesus, he receives "everlasting

> *Consequently,*
> *seeking revival is not*
> *seeking something;*
> *rather seeking*
> *revival is seeking*
> Someone.

life." However, eternal life is not *something* but rather *Someone*.
Jesus said in John 14:6, "I am . . . *the life*." The word *life* is from
zoe, which is the noun form of the verb *zao* in *anazao*. Jesus
said in John 17:3, "And this is life eternal, that they may know
[experientially] thee the only true God, and Jesus Christ." In
I John 1:2, Jesus is referred to as "*that eternal life*." First John
5:20 says, "His Son Jesus Christ. This is the true God, and
eternal life." Therefore Christ's life is *the Eternal Life*. Christ's
life applied by the Holy Spirit to the believer is *the Life* of life
again. Thus in the most essential sense, *the defining essence of
revival is a restoration to spiritual life*. This definition, however,
may be tailored according to the extent of one's focus. The
end of this chapter will discuss in detail the extent of revival.

However, for defining purposes major levels of extent will be mentioned here.

Personal Revival

On the individual level, revival accesses the Eternal Life who indwells the believer as the Abundant Life. This reality of revival individually is essentially the Spirit-filled life. The Spirit-filled life is the Spirit filling the believer with the life of Christ. "The Holy Ghost, which is in you" (I Cor. 6:19), is "Christ in you" (Col. 1:27) and therefore "Christ, who is our life" (Col. 3:4). This reality is the provision for "I live; yet not I, but Christ liveth in me" by "faith" (Gal. 2:20). Then "to me to live is Christ" (Phil. 1:21). This is the very essence of revival because revival accesses the Eternal Life as the Abundant Life and is therefore a restoration to spiritual life or life in the Spirit. It is the eternal life of Christ in the believer accessed as the animating life principle to one's personality. This is genuine life again.

Consequently, seeking revival is not seeking *something*; rather seeking revival is seeking *Someone*. Many enjoy reading revival history. At times revival accounts are quite dramatic. However, there is a subtle danger in this. If one is not careful, he may end up seeking the sensational. While one may revel in the wonderful works of God from a motivational standpoint, the works are not to be sought as such but rather the Worker Himself. To seek the sensational reveals an entertainment motive which God cannot bless. This wrong focus causes delay among those who seek revival. Those who may be somewhat disappointed at this clarification reveal that they think the sensational satisfies. But only Jesus satisfies! Thus believers must seek *Him*, not *it*.

The works (what revival *does*) will vary according to the needs involved. What is essential is the Worker. Therefore seeking revival is seeking God. More specifically, seeking revival is seeking Christ, who is *the Life* of "life again." And therefore knowing revival is actually knowing Christ, and experiencing revival is experiencing Christ—in the fullness of His life (Phil. 3:10).

Basic to revival is the understanding that the Christian life is essentially a *life*. The Christian life is not merely a set of doctrines and a particular lifestyle. The Christian life is a person. Jesus Christ is *the Christian Life*. Therefore no one can live the Christian life but Christ. In other words, the Christian life is not just hard; it is impossible—for man. But when someone is born again, Christ indwells that person to impart to him His divine life. Then the believer can live, yet not him but Christ in him, *the Christian Life*—by faith (Gal. 2:20). Christ moves in to the believer to live His life, not the man's. This is not His life *instead* of the man's, but His life *through* the man's.

When a believer lives his life by self-will and self-dependence, he veils Christ's life. But when a believer denies his life by denying self-will and self-dependence, he unveils Christ's life. In scriptural terminology when a believer saves his life, he loses it; but when he loses his life, he finds it (Matt. 16:25; Mark 8:35; Luke 9:24; John 12:25). The key is in understanding that the word *life* is from *psuche,* meaning "soul" or "self." Therefore when a believer saves his "life" (self) by living the "self-life," even if it is self living for God ("consecrated self," which is nonetheless "self"), he loses it because all that is of the self-life will be incinerated as wood, hay, and stubble at the judgment seat of Christ (I Cor. 3:11–15). But when a believer loses his "life" (self) by yielding to Christ's life, he finds it animated by Christ's own life and thus becoming the gold, silver, and precious stones that will endure the judgment seat fires. For only God meets the standard of God.

When a believer saves his life, he loses it. But when he loses or releases it, he finds Christ's life, which is the core of true discipleship. Yet true discipleship is revival. It is re-discovering *the Christian Life.* For when one yields to the will of Christ and depends on His power, Christ, *the Christian Life,* animates and energizes his personality. The revived life individually is therefore the Spirit-filled life. It is a restoration to Christ as one's life. For the Spirit-filled life is the Spirit filling the believer with the life of Christ. The Spirit through the human spirit fills the human soul (life) with the life of Christ. So in a sense revival occurs in the soul; yet it is accomplished by the Spirit. It is *the Life (zoe)* animating the believer's life *(psuche).* It is *spiritual life.*

God used Andrew Murray to help lead the Great Revival of 1860 in South Africa. It is no accident that Murray wrote his classic work *Abide in Christ,* a book on the Spirit-filled life, as a result of what he himself learned during the revival. The revived life is what is accessed through abiding in Christ.

Revival accesses Christ's life. Therefore, *personal revival is a restoration to spiritual life in the sense of a saint being restored to the Spirit-filled life.* This defining sense is the narrowest definition of revival, for it addresses only what revival is on the individual level. The definition can and will broaden as other factors are considered.

Corporate Revival

When the individuals in a local church or perhaps a subgroup within a local church simultaneously experience revival, the restoration to spiritual life refers to more than just the Spirit-filled life of individual believers to the healthy "body-life" of that particular body of Christ. The group as a whole is restored to life in the Spirit, where Christ is acknowledged as Lord and the Spirit is depended upon for life in the corporate function of the body. The spiritual gifts of the members then operate unhindered as believers walk in the Spirit. Therefore, *corporate revival is a restoration to spiritual life in the sense of the saints being restored to the Spirit-led and Spirit-enabled function of a body of believers.*

A Revival of Religion

The terminology of a *revival of religion* was used frequently in the Great Awakenings of the past. The reference focuses on the awakening work of the Spirit among the lost during times of revival among the saints. Although in the narrow sense of the word, one must be "vived" before he can be "revived," there is a broader sense in which a lost man, who, because of Adam's sin, is alienated from the life of God, yet may be restored to the life of God through the new birth. Therefore, *a revival of religion is a restoration to spiritual life in the sense of the unsaved being restored to the original plan of God indwelling man.*

General Revival

The terminology *general revival* refers to times when revival among the saints and a revival of religion among the lost become, in greater or lesser degrees, pervasive among a given people or across a given land in a continuing fashion. Therefore, *general revival is a restoration to spiritual life in the sense of a people in a broad area being restored to the life of God.*

The definition of *revival* may broaden further when the other phases of revival are considered, especially the outpouring of the Spirit. Later chapters will address this broader sense of revival. However, when considering the concept of revival in people, revival is a restoration to spiritual life. Ultimately, whether considering individuals or a corporate grouping, *revival is a restoration to life in, through, and by the Spirit.* In other words, *revival is a restoration to the life of God.*

THE DEFINING EVIDENCE OF REVIVAL IS A RESTORATION TO SPIRITUAL LIVING

The *essence* of revival is what revival *is*. The *evidence* of revival is what revival *does*. If the defining essence of revival is a restoration to spiritual life, then the defining evidence of revival is a restoration to spiritual living. Since the essence of revival is a restoration to Christ's life, then the evidence of revival is a restoration to the living out of Christ's life through the believer and in the broader sense through the church.

It is no accident that the two concepts of the essence of revival and the evidence of revival are combined into an oft-repeated phrase found throughout revival literature: "the Spirit-filled life for holiness and service." *The Spirit-filled life* refers to the essence of revival, and *for holiness and service* refers to the evidence of revival. This may be manifested on both individual and corporate levels. But what is true holiness and what is true service?

Holiness

Holiness is love to God in being what one ought to be. The key is the Spirit-filled life—for holiness. Personal holiness is not merely going through a set of moral motions. Unsaved moralists can do that. Personal holiness is accessing the Person of holiness, Christ *in* the believer (the essence of revival), for holy living, Christ *through* the believer (the evidence of revival). When one accesses the Holy Life, Christ Himself, he discovers that Christ is patient, Christ is pure, Christ is unselfish, Christ is not irritable, Christ does not make abrasive comments, Christ does not have any fleshly addictions, and so forth. Holiness is the fruit of the Spirit, which is the character of Christ. When one accesses Christ, he accesses *the Victorious Life.*

Truly, there is only one victorious life—His name is Jesus! How can it be otherwise? Historically, the phrases "the Spirit-filled life," "the Victorious Life," "the Higher Life," and "the Deeper Life" all meant the same thing—the Life of Christ. Some of these phrases have occasionally had other ideas attached to them by "fringe" groups over the years. However, their original usages all referred to simply accessing the indwelling life of Christ as one's life. Therefore the provision for victory is perfect—His name is Jesus! Sadly the faith-access to this provision by God's people is imperfect. But the provision is the holy life of Christ Himself.

For example, missionary Ruth Paxson testified of the following:

After a revival in a mission station in China during which many of the Christians had received the fullness of the Holy Spirit, one missionary wrote, "Our hospital is no more like it used to be. There is *perfect harmony* among all the hospital workers from servants on up. All do faithful work. I never have to reprove any of them. I even never have to tell servants what to do. All know their work, and do it faithfully." Filled with the Holy Spirit, both the manner and the motive of every servant's work will be such as to make for harmony [emphasis original].[7]

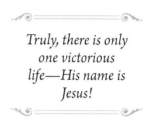

Truly, there is only one victorious life—His name is Jesus!

This is the evidence of the holy, and therefore, victorious life of Christ. But holiness is not an end in itself. Holiness opens the way for empowered service.

Service

Service is love to man in doing what one ought to do. As holiness has to do with *being* right, service has to do with *doing* right. Again the key is the Spirit-filled life—for service. Service is not just mimicking good actions, because service in the strength of the flesh lacks carrying power and profits nothing (John 6:63). Personal service is accessing the Person of service, Christ *in* the believer (the essence of revival), for powerful serving, Christ *through* the believer (the evidence of revival). When Christ is yielded to and depended upon, He frees the believer to witness of Him, and the Spirit convicts the hearers. Christ has a burning passion to declare the good news. He is the master winner of souls, and He lives in every believer. Revival accesses "Christ in you" and His fervency for the lost.

This is one of the reasons that seasons of revival among the saints are generally followed by fervent evangelism and seasons of harvest among the lost.

When a believer is restored to spiritual life (the essence of revival) and restored to spiritual living (the evidence of revival), he is brought back to normal. The Spirit-filled life for holiness and service is the normal Christian life. In Canada there is an auto mechanics' garage called "Auto Revival." It is rather interesting to see the word *revival* connected with a car. But the meaning is clear. If someone's car is broken down and needs fixing, he can bring it and it will get fixed. It does not mean that the car will be made into a "supercar," but it does mean it will be brought back to normal working condition.

Physically, when someone almost drowns, and a rescuer restores respiration to the near-dead person so that he revives, he does not become superhuman; rather he comes back to normal. Likewise, spiritually, when a Christian is languishing from unbelief and then is revived, he does not become a "super-Christian"; he simply comes back to normal.[8] He is restored to spiritual life and spiritual living.

The problem today is that many of God's people are so accustomed to the subnormal way things are that they think revival is extraordinary, when in reality revival is just coming back to normal. The revived life is the normal Christian life, and God's people must not be content with a subnormal form of religion. As the reality of the revived life ought to be the norm for believers individually, seasons of refreshing from the presence of the Lord ought to be the norm for the church corporately. An anemic church thought of as the norm is an insult to Jesus Christ. The church ought to be functioning in the fullness of Christ's life.

When churches are filled with worldliness or mimic the form of godliness while denying its very power, they are subnormal and in need of being restored to normal. This affects Evangelicals, who in some cases are compromised with the world (self-indulgent) and yet condemn some Fundamentalists for their "letter without the Spirit" Christianity. It also affects Fundamentalists, who in some cases are "formal ritualists" (self-dependent) and yet condemn some Evangelicals for their compromised Christianity. In both cases the real answer is to be restored to the norm of Christ's energizing life.

THE DEFINING EXTENT OF REVIVAL IS THE REALM OF INFLUENCE

The matter of extent is vital to forming a proper conception of revival. Building upon the broad categories of revival mentioned earlier, more specific subcategories may be helpful to the understanding.

Personal Revival

First, there is *personal revival*. For example, a preacher said that he used to think everyone had to have besetting sins until they went to heaven. This, of course, gives the ground for the besetting sins. Then with excitement he exclaimed that he had been reading books on the Spirit-filled life by authors such as Andrew Murray. He went on to say, "I'm almost afraid to say it, but I have experienced victory over certain sins that I did not think was possible this side of heaven!" This is a beautiful testimony of real transformation through personal revival. Another preacher wrote that after four months from having his eyes opened to the reality of the indwelling Holy Spirit accessed by faith, his life was truly being changed. He said that scriptural passages that he had studied for years were coming alive. He even commented, "It's as if all things have become new!" This is *life again* on the personal level.

When one person experiences restoration to spiritual life bringing peace, purity, and power—revival has come. At that point it is a matter of revival spreading.

Corporate Revival

Second, there is *small group revival*. Sometimes a few within a larger group experience real revival. Interestingly, personal revival and often small group revival precedes greater revival. The personal and small group revivals prepare the intercessors to intercede with faith for greater blessing. The intercessors then access the blessing for others who will not access it for themselves. History amply provides numerous illustrations of this principle.

Third, there is *church-wide revival* in which the majority of a church together experiences a season of refreshing. This revitalizes the church body. Historically, many churches have experienced "their Pentecost" and were propelled into a new dimension with God. The Moravian Revival of 1727 is a classic example of this powerful reality.[9]

A Revival of Religion

Fourth, there is *community-wide revival*. An example of this occurred in 1735 in Northampton, Massachusetts. Jonathan Edwards claimed that the average conversation of people in the streets of the town was about God. The whole community was shaken by an awareness of God.

Fifth, there is *regional revival* in which a number of communities within a particular region are affected by the moving of God's Spirit. The Lewis Awakening (1949–1953) is a good example of a regional revival. The Isle of Lewis, located off the northwest coast of Scotland, has two major towns with a number of villages. Duncan Campbell came in 1949 for what he thought was going to be a ten-day meeting in the village of Barvas. But God came in reviving power, and Campbell preached throughout the island largely for the next three years.

General Revival

Sixth, there is *national revival*. The Welsh Revival of 1904–1905 is a good example. Nearly every part of the principality of Wales knew the undeniable sense of the presence and working of God. Another example is the revival that took place from 1857–1858 in the United States. Revival historian J. Edwin Orr wrote that "the influence of the Revival was felt everywhere in the nation. It first captured the great cities, but it also spread through every town and village and country hamlet. It swamped schools and colleges. It affected all classes regardless of condition . . . It seemed to many that the fruits of Pentecost had been repeated a thousandfold."[10]

Finally, there is *international revival*. J. Edwin Orr documents a wave of revival that impacted at least 57 nations from 1901 to 1913, including a national revival in the United States in 1906. Many of the well-known names from that time period, such as Billy Sunday in America and Gypsy Smith in Great Britain, were riding this tidal wave of blessing.[11]

J. Edwin Orr summarizes the essence, the evidence, and the extent of revival with the following:

An Evangelical Awakening is a movement of the Holy Spirit bringing about a revival of New Testament Christianity in the Church of Christ and in its related community. Such an awakening may change in a significant way an individual only; or it may affect a larger group of believers; or it may move a congregation, or the churches of a city or district, or the whole body of believers throughout a country or a continent; or indeed the larger body of believers throughout the world. [12]

Whether revival is personal or corporate, it is the same dynamic. This truth must be understood in order to have a proper conception of revival. When revival comes to one person, revival has come. Then it is a matter of asking God to spread the revival by crying out, "Wilt thou not revive us again: that thy people may rejoice in thee?"

Summary of the Phases of Revival:

The REVIVAL JOURNEY

QUESTION FOR
THOUGHT:
Since revival is "life
again," what is the way
into this blessing?

Chapter Two

BROKENNESS: THE WAY INTO BLESSING

Phase Four

*J*onathan Goforth writes of the Manchurian Revival of 1908: *"During the four days that I was at Hungtung the Spirit of Burning was very much in evidence. Hidden sins were continually brought out . . . men and women everywhere began to break down under the conviction of sin."*[1]

This is just one example of a multitude. When the "Spirit of Judgment" and the "Spirit of Burning" moved through the audience, many responded in great brokenness. This breaking led people into revival blessing.

The principle of brokenness opening the way to blessing is found repeatedly in Scripture. Psalm 34:18 states, "The Lord is nigh unto them that are of a broken heart; and saveth such as be of a contrite spirit." Isaiah 57:15 records, "For thus saith the high and lofty One that inhabiteth eternity, whose name is Holy; I dwell in the high and holy place with him, also that is of a contrite and humble spirit,

> *Since brokenness is the way into blessing, believers must live in brokenness before God and man.*

to revive the spirit of the humble, and to revive the heart of the contrite ones." Since brokenness is the way into blessing, believers must live in brokenness before God and man.

What exactly is brokenness? How does one know that it leads to blessing? The answers may be found by investigating the key words and concepts in a topical exposition of pertinent Scripture and noting their specific promises.

THE PRICE OF BROKENNESS

The majority of this study revolves around discerning what brokenness *is*.

Key Defining Words

The Scripture incorporates three primary words in the Old Testament with parallel words and concepts in the New Testament.

Broken

First, the word *broken* (*shabar*) occurs as a verb 147 times in the Old Testament. The meaning of the word is "break" or "break in pieces." One verb form is often used of God dealing with the nations. Another verb form is used of destroying idols, where the nuance is literally "to smash to smithereens."[2] Figuratively, with some verb forms the word means "to be broken of heart."[3]

In the figurative sense, the verb is used with various verb forms in several key revival contexts. As noted in Psalm 34:18, "The Lord is nigh unto them that are of *broken* heart." Psalm 51:17 says, "The sacrifices of God are a *broken* spirit: a *broken* and a contrite heart, O God, thou wilt not despise." Psalm 147:3 affirms that "He healeth the *broken* in heart." Isaiah 61:1 states that "the Spirit of the Lord God is upon me; because the Lord hath anointed me to . . . bind up the *brokenhearted*." Similarly in Ezekiel 34:16, God says, "I will seek that which was lost, and bring again that which was driven away, and will bind up that which was *broken* and will strengthen that which was sick."

In all of these contexts the major thought of the word *broken* is to be broken of heart or heartbroken.

A New Testament parallel can be found in Luke 4:18, where Christ quotes from Isaiah 61:1, "The Spirit of the Lord is upon me, because . . . he hath sent me to heal the *brokenhearted*." This is the only time in the New Testament that the word *broken* or *brokenhearted* is used in a context with revival overtones, although the concept is used elsewhere. The word Jesus uses actually combines two Greek words: *suntribo*, meaning to "shatter, smash, crush,"[4] and *kardia,* referring to the heart. Again the idea is to be broken of heart or heartbroken.

Contrite

Second, the word *contrite* (*dakka'* and *daka'*) occurs three times in the Old Testament as an adjective meaning "crushed."[5] It is used 23 times as a verb with various forms being incorporated. The KJV translates the verb as "crush" in Lamentations 3:34; "break in pieces" [the oppressor] in Psalm 72:4; "humbled" in Jeremiah 44:10; "broken" in Psalm 89:10; and "bruised" in Isaiah 53:5 in the phrase "he was bruised for our iniquities."

The word occurs in several revival contexts. Again Psalm 34:18 states, "And saveth such as be of a *contrite* spirit." Also Psalm 51:17 says in the context of confession, "A broken and a *contrite* heart, O God, thou wilt not despise." Then Isaiah 57:15 declares, "For thus saith the high and lofty One that inhabiteth eternity, whose name is Holy; I dwell in the high and holy place, with him also that is of a *contrite* and humble spirit, to revive the spirit of the humble, and to revive the heart of the *contrite* ones." Isaiah 66:2 incorporates a similar sense but uses a different word (*nakeh*) when God says, "But to this man will I look, even to him that is poor and of a *contrite* spirit, and trembleth at my word."

The major thought of the word *contrite* in these contexts is to be crushed in heart, making the usage synonymous with being broken of heart.

Although the New Testament does not use the word *contrite,* the word *poor* is used once in a similar sense in Matthew 5:3, "Blessed are the *poor* in spirit."

But what does it mean to be broken or crushed in heart? The third primary word often used parallel with *broken* or *contrite* provides more understanding.

Humble

In the Old Testament the word *humble* (*shaphal* and *shaphel*) is used multiple times as an adjective and as a verb. The basic meaning is "low."[6] In the physical sense, Leviticus 13–14 connects this being "low" with leprosy. The word is used frequently with God's warning to bring low or abase the proud and with His promise to lift up or exalt the humble (lowly). In this sense to be humble is to be honest, for honesty recognizes the "lowliness" of one's person before God. It is an accurate assessment that agrees with God's perspective. It is this spiritual sense that must be cultivated.

Revival contexts include Psalm 138:6, "Though the Lord be high, yet hath he respect unto the *lowly*." Also Isaiah 57:15 states that God dwells "in the high and holy place, with him also that is of a contrite and *humble* spirit, to revive the spirit of the *humble*, and to revive the heart of the contrite ones."

The classic II Chronicles 7:14 uses a different word (*kana'*): "If my people, which are called by my name, shall *humble* themselves, and pray, and seek my face, and turn from their wicked ways; then will I hear from heaven, and will forgive their sin, and will heal their land." This word is used most often dealing with subjection. However, Leviticus 26:41 speaks of God remembering those whose "hearts be *humbled*." In these two contexts the meaning is basically the same as *shaphel* noted above. One other synonym (*'anah*) does not seem to take on the revival sense.[7]

The New Testament affirms three times that the one who exalts himself will be abased and the one who humbles himself will be exalted (Matt. 23:12; Luke 14:11; 18:14). Twice the New Testament explains that "God resisteth the proud" but "giveth grace unto the humble" (James 4:6; I Pet. 5:5). Twice this explanation is followed with the admonishment to "humble" oneself before the Lord that the Lord may lift up the humbled (James 4:10; I Pet. 5:6).

Between the adjective *humble* (*tapeinos*) in James 4:6, "God . . . giveth grace unto the *humble*," and the verb *humble* (*tapeinoo*) in James 4:10, "*Humble* yourselves in the sight of the Lord, and he shall lift you up," is a helpful description of what it means to be humble: "Submit yourselves therefore to God. Resist the devil, and he will flee from you. Draw nigh to God, and he will draw nigh to you. Cleanse your hands, ye sinners; and purify your hearts, ye double minded. Be afflicted, and mourn, and weep: let your laughter be turned to mourning, and your joy to heaviness" (James 4:7–9). It is significant to note that when James 4:10 then commands, "Humble yourselves in the sight of the Lord,"

> *To be* broken *(broken of heart) or* contrite *(crushed in heart) is to be* humble *(honest in spirit). Genuine honesty involves* confession *(honesty regarding sin and the need for divine cleansing),* surrender *(honesty regarding self and the need for divine leadership and enablement), and* faith *(honesty regarding Christ and the provision of divine sufficiency).*

the imperative is in the passive voice, which indicates "Allow yourselves to be humbled."

The major thought of humility in both the Old and the New Testaments is honesty. A humble spirit assesses matters accurately in true honesty. Honesty understands how "low" one actually is apart from God's enablement. Humility recognizes the error of one's ways and the need for divine deliverance.

In summary, while the three primary words all have individual nuances, they are all used interchangeably in the revival contexts. Essentially they convey the same basic idea. To be *broken* (broken of heart) or *contrite* (crushed in heart) is to be *humble* (honest in spirit). Genuine honesty involves confession (honesty regarding sin and the need for divine cleansing), surrender (honesty regarding self and the need for divine leadership and enablement), and faith (honesty regarding Christ and the provision of divine sufficiency).

However, this message of brokenness is an unpopular message. People are not looking for books on how to mourn and weep.[8] In a world promoting self-esteem, an honest assessment of one's self does not seem to fit the paradigm. Rather the desire is to find bestsellers that make one feel "warm and fuzzy."

In her helpful book *Brokenness: The Heart God Revives*, Nancy Leigh DeMoss elaborates on this:

> Our culture is obsessed with being whole and feeling good. That drive even affects the way we view the Christian life. We want a "painless Pentecost"; we want a

"laughing" revival. We want gain without pain; we want the resurrection without going through the grave; we want life without experiencing death; we want a crown without going by way of the cross. But in God's economy, the way up is down.

You and I will never meet God in revival until we first meet Him in brokenness.[9]

Now that the key defining words have been surveyed, the foundation has been laid to build the key defining concepts.

Key Defining Concepts

To expand one's understanding of brokenness, wrong conceptions must be confronted so that right conceptions may be clearly understood.

What Brokenness Is Not

Some think brokenness is walking around with a dejected look and always having a downcast countenance. But true brokenness brings release and joy. Some consider brokenness to be a morbid introspection where one is always looking inward to discover something that needs to be confessed. But oversensitive consciences lead to "over confession." In reality introspection is a self-focus and is therefore a form of pride. It is a false humility. True brokenness is a God-focus. The psalmist prayed, "Search me, O God"—not "Search me, O me!" Some think brokenness is going through a severe trial of some sort, whether physical, financial, relational, or otherwise, as a type of punishment. But this is the thinking of meritorious penance. While it is true that God may use a trial as chastening to arrest one's attention and bring him to brokenness, it is possible to go through a trial without being broken. Simply going through a trial does not equal brokenness. True brokenness responds rightly in a trial. Some believe brokenness to be of necessity an emotional experience. However, it is possible to shed many tears without being broken. True brokenness may or may not be accompanied with tears.[10]

> *Confession is getting honest about the wickedness of one's sin—accurately, thoroughly, and without making any excuses.*

Most of these misconceptions regarding brokenness involve the idea of gaining favor with God through some type of meritorious penance. But Psalm 51:16–17 clarifies this: "For thou desirest not sacrifice; else would I give it: thou delightest not in burnt offering. The sacrifices of God are a broken spirit." This statement indicates that brokenness is not jumping over some type of spiritual hurdle to gain favor with God.

What Brokenness Is

Brokenness involves three realizations and their correlating responses.

Seeing One's Sin as Exceedingly Sinful: The Response of Confession

The first realization of brokenness is seeing the wickedness of one's sin and responding with the cry of confession. In fact, the "broken and contrite heart" of Psalm 51 is in the context of confession. David cried out, "For I acknowledge my transgressions: and my sin is ever before me" (v. 3). First John 1:9 states that "if we confess our sins, he is faithful and just to forgive us our sins, and to cleanse us from all unrighteousness." The word *confess* (*homologeo*) means "to say the same thing."[11] The implication in the context is to say the same thing as God says about one's sin. This demands seeing one's sin as God sees it. When this is the case, sin is seen as exceedingly sinful. Confession is getting honest about the wickedness of one's sin—accurately, thoroughly, and without making any excuses.

However, since the heart is deceitful (Jer. 17:9) and is only known truly by the Lord (Jer. 17:10), it is vital to look to the Lord for a glimpse into one's heart. For example, in Psalm 139: 23–24, the psalmist prayed, "Search me, O God, and know my heart: try me, and know my thoughts: And see if there be any wicked way in me, and lead me in the way everlasting." When one sees what God sees, then he can say what God says. At that point the confession can be truly accurate.

It follows that confession must be thorough, dealing with all that God reveals as sinful. Surface confession does not bring full relief. General confession leads to spiritual dullness. But specific confession that is thorough leads to spiritual cleansing.

Furthermore, genuine confession is getting honest about one's sin without making any excuses. The tendency of humanity is to shift the blame to others or to circumstances as the reason for one's sin. This blame shifting attempts to justify one's wrongdoing. It seeks to cover up one's sin. This "cover-up" is walking in darkness. Pride is at the root of this tree of concealment. The false notion comes from thinking, "I'm not that bad. That wrong action or those wrong words were not really me. The situation or that person drew it out of me." But the reality is that the situation or other person simply exposed what was already in someone. Confession is saying, "I'm that bad. I'm that wicked. That is what I am." Confession is painful honesty without any attempt to justify one's sin.

The extent of the sin determines the necessary extent of the confession. Generally speaking, private sin demands private confession (I John 1:9). Personal sin demands personal confession (James 5:16; Matt. 5:23–24). Personal sin is sinning against another person and that other person knows it (which will generally be obvious). Public sin demands public confession based on the same principle (James 5:16; Matt. 5:23–24).

When sin is seen as exceedingly sinful, it will also be seen as ultimately sinning against God. David confessed, "Against thee, thee only, have I sinned, and done this evil in thy sight" (Ps. 51:4). True confession is concerned about having dishonored God.

In the corporate setting, brokenness often breeds brokenness. Often one person's honesty is used of the Spirit to convince others to be honest. Corporate brokenness is a powerful scene. For example, the following is an account from Jonathan Goforth during the Manchurian Revival:

Presently a lady missionary, whose bursts of bad temper were notorious throughout the mission, rose and in great brokenness prayed that God would remove the hindering thing from her life. Right after her another lady missionary confessed to her lack of love for the people to whom she had come to minister, and pleaded that to her, too, grace might be given and the obstacle taken away. Then Miss L____, the Chinese head-teacher of the Girls' School, whom all thought to be about as perfect a Christian as it was possible to find, confessed in tears to her selfishness and unworthiness of the example which she was setting to her girls.

By this time Dr. L.____ was completely broken up. "O heavenly Father," he cried now, "forgive Thy sinning servant. I have spoken unadvisedly with my lips and hurt a Chinese brother. Thou knowest, O God, how that a long time ago Thy servant Moses spoke unadvisedly with his lips, and Thou didst punish him by not permitting him to enter the Promised Land. But only Moses was punished; the people did not suffer for his sin. The people were permitted to enter the land of blessing. Now, therefore, O God, punish Thy servant before Thee in like manner; but let not Thy people be hindered from obtaining the promised blessing."

Scarcely had the doctor ended when a man fell to the floor of the church with a terrible cry. It was a huffy evangelist. The next moment a man in another part of the audience was affected in precisely the same way. This time it was the Chinese principal of the Boys' School, one who had been undermining Dr. L____'s authority and endeavouring to work up rebellion among the students. In a few minutes men and women all over the building were falling on their knees and confessing their sins. One of the older boys cried, "Get down on your knees," and they all went down. On my left were the girls. Suddenly, without a word of command, like a wind sweeping over a field of grain, they, too, fell on their knees. Soon it seemed to me as if every last man, woman, and child was on the floor of that church crying for mercy.[12]

Seeing One's Self as Exceedingly Willful: The Response of Surrender

The second realization of brokenness is seeing the willfulness of one's self and responding with the choice of surrender. When someone waves the white flag of surrender, it is a crisis for it means he is giving up. Surrender is giving up one's will because of giving in to another's will. However, this "giving up" is not passivity. Surrender in the life of the believer is not willing oneself into "will-lessness," for that is passivity, which is the devil's playground. Surrender is not idle passivity but active cooperation—a glad cooperation with the will of Christ. Surrender is yielding up self-will by yielding to God's will. This surrender of the will is a part of brokenness.

A horse that is broken does not mean a horse that no longer has a will; it means a horse whose will is yielded to his rider's will.

For the believer to be broken, what is it that must be broken? To be contrite, what is it that must be crushed? The answer is self-will. Whatever is in the way of "not I, but Christ" must be given up. Whatever one is saying no to God about must be given up. This is the point of breaking.

Self-will includes two major areas: self-will regarding the *leadership* of one's life and self-will regarding the *enablement* of one's life. Christ is both the Lord (leadership) and Life (enablement) of the believer. Therefore a broken believer

> *Brokenness brings one to the realization that he is weak and always will be weak this side of heaven.*

surrenders up his will as he surrenders to Christ's will, and he surrenders up his strength as he surrenders to Christ's strength.

The first area revolves around *leadership*. Broken believers stop saying no to the leadership of Christ and start saying yes. This may involve giving up some aspect of worldliness such as media choices, fashion choices, or music choices. It may involve giving up a relationship that is not God's will. It may involve giving up an ambition in life that is not God's will. Some matters may be obvious, but others may not be so clear. In fact, a real test of the brokenness of a believer is in the areas that good men debate over, but the Holy Spirit guides that believer to give up that issue. True brokenness yields to the lordship of Christ through the leadership of the Spirit.

Before Douglas Brown could be used of God in the East Anglia Revival, which began in England in 1921, he had to be broken of self-will regarding not wanting to be in mission work (itinerant ministry).

Preaching from II Chronicles 7:14, Douglas Brown illustrated the words, "If my people shall humble themselves . . ." from his own experience. He said it had taken four months for that truth to get home to him, even though he had been a minister of the Gospel for twenty-six years . . . . The rest of the story is best told in his own words:

"God laid hold of me in the midst of a Sunday evening service, and He nearly broke my heart while I was preaching. I went back to my vestry, and locked the door, and threw myself down on the hearthrug in front of the vestry fireplace broken-hearted. Why? I do not know. My church was filled. I loved my people, and I believe my people loved me. I do not say they ought to, but they did. I was as happy there as I could be. I had never known a Sunday there for fifteen years without conversions. That night I went home and went straight up to my study. My wife came to tell me that supper was ready and was waiting. 'You must not [delay] supper for me,' I said. 'What is the matter?' she asked. 'I have got a broken heart,' was my reply. It was worth-while having a broken heart for Jesus to mend it. I had no supper that night. Christ laid his hand on a proud minister and told him that he had not gone far enough, that there were reservations in his surrender, and He wanted him to do a piece of work that he had been trying to evade. I knew what He meant. All November that struggle went on, but I would not give way; I knew God was right, and I knew I was wrong. I knew what it would mean for me, and I was not prepared to pay the price. Then

Christmas time came, and all the joy round about seemed to mock me. I knew what Jesus wanted. . . . The struggle went on, and I said to the Lord, 'You know that is not my work. I will pray for anyone else who does it, but please do not give it to me, it will kill me. I cannot get into the pulpit and plead with people. It is against my temperament, and You made me.'"

"All through January God wrestled with me. There is a love that will not let us go. Glory be to God! . . . It was in February 1921, after four months of struggle, that there came the crisis. Oh, how patient God is! On the Saturday night I wrote out my resignation to my church, and it was marked with my own tears. I loved the church, but I felt that if I could not be holy I would be honest; I felt that I could not go on preaching while I had a contention with God. That night . . . As I went out of my bedroom door in the early hours of the morning, I stumbled over my dog . . . .

"Then something happened. I found myself in the loving embrace of Christ forever and ever; and all power and joy and all blessedness rolled in like a deluge. . . . That was two o'clock in the morning. God had waited four months for a man like me; and I said, 'Lord Jesus, I know what you want; You want me to go into mission work. I love Thee more than I dislike that.' I did not hear any rustling of angels' wings. I did not see any sudden light."[13]

Within days after this surrender to the Spirit's leadership, Douglas Brown went to Lowestoft, England for a mission (meeting). God sent a mighty revival that spread to northeast England and part of Scotland, lasting from March 1921 well into 1922.

The second area of self-will revolves around *enablement.* Some people say, "I surrender all and I'm going to do it!" However, this thinking reveals a lack of surrender to God's power. Brokenness brings one to the realization that he is weak and always will be weak this side of heaven. This realization responds in full surrender: giving up on one's strength, which is actually weakness, and resting in the enablement of the indwelling Christ. The "poor in spirit" recognize that they are utterly destitute and therefore utterly dependent on the riches of Christ's grace. This may be the hardest lesson for servants of God to learn.

Many are the ministers of the Gospel who have been frustrated by doing God's work in the strength of the flesh. Yet this futility of the flesh has brought many to the end of self, which is the beginning of God. When self-dependence is confessed as arrogant sin and God-dependence is embraced, self-will regarding enablement is broken.

Brokenness is the breaking of self-will regarding both leadership and enablement by surrendering to the leadership of Christ and to the enablement of the Holy Spirit. Therefore brokenness is more than confession of sin. True brokenness also involves the giving up of the self-will behind the sin.

Furthermore, some confess their guilt (in the name of confessing their sin) because they do not like the way they feel, but in reality they still desire the sin. Therefore when temptation arises, they gladly take the sin again because they have not dealt with the root of self-will. They have not yet let go of the sin. Some even ask God to take away the sin, but they do not let go of it and wonder why they do not receive victory. But God does not play "tug-of-war" with people. True brokenness says, "God, I give this sin up. I do not reserve the right to ever take it again. But God, this is beyond me. I need supernatural deliverance." This is surrendering to God's leadership and enablement. This is the breaking of self-will. But this is the brokenness that accesses divine deliverance.

Seeing One's Savior as Exceedingly Faithful: The Response of Faith

The third realization of brokenness is seeing the faithfulness of the Savior and responding with the claim of faith. Essentially, faith is God-dependence based on God's words. Brokenness depends on God to forgive, to cleanse, and to restore to fellowship. When a believer comes clean with God through genuine confession and surrender, "He [God] is faithful and just to forgive." This involves a release from what is owed, a cleansing through the power of the blood of Jesus, and a restoration to "fellowship" (I John 1:7, 9). When a believer is broken before the Lord who knows all, God "cleans him all up" and restores him to communion with Himself. The psalmist cried out, "Create in me a clean heart, O God; and renew a right spirit within me" (Ps. 51:10). Once the cry for mercy has truly been uttered and the choice of surrender has truly been made, God in His faithfulness cleanses and restores. Then the broken believer can claim in faith the "clean heart" and "right spirit." He can actually know he is clean based on God's promise, regardless of how he feels. In his classic *The Calvary Road,* Roy Hession states, "We can't be more right with God than what the blood of Jesus makes us when we call sin *sin.*"[14] The broken believer therefore claims by faith a clean heart.

When John George Govan, who was later used of God to train Duncan Campbell and many others in revival work, surrendered his youthful ambitions, which he knew were not the will of God, he walked out of the church and said to a friend, "I have a clean heart, I have trusted the Lord, and I know He has done it, though I don't feel any different." This claim revealed faith regarding a clean heart. Later he wrote, "When I got home that night and went down before the Lord, then I knew the difference. The glory of God flooded my soul, and it has been different ever since."[15]

THE PROMISE FOR BROKENNESS

After discerning what brokenness *is,* it is vital to also discern what brokenness *accesses.* Brokenness is the way into blessing. But what is the blessing?

Psalm 34:18 promises that "the *Lord is nigh* unto them that are of a broken heart; and *saveth* such as be of a contrite spirit." Here the promise is the nearness of the Lord Himself and His deliverance. The focus is on the very presence of the Lord and the deliverance that that presence brings. Brokenness accesses the reviving presence of the Lord. God's reviving presence is the heart of revival. It brings life to those who need life again.

Isaiah 57:15 promises, "For thus saith the high and lofty One that inhabiteth eternity, whose name is Holy; I dwell in the high and holy place, with him also that is of a contrite and humble spirit, *to revive* the spirit of the humble, and *to revive* the heart of the contrite ones." The promise for brokenness is revival! It is amazing that God dwells with the contrite and humble for the purpose of reviving their hearts.

Psalm 51:17 promises that "a broken and a contrite heart, O God, thou wilt not despise." Rather than despising the broken and contrite heart, God revives it. Psalm 138:6 promises, "Though the Lord be high, yet hath he respect unto the lowly." Psalm 147:3 promises, "He healeth the broken in heart, and bindeth up their wounds." Truly brokenness is the way into blessing! Samuel Chadwick states, "It is a wonder what God can do with a broken heart, if He gets all the pieces."

The promise is also found in the New Testament: "God resisteth the proud [the unbroken], but giveth grace [Spirit-enablement—the life of revival] unto the humble [the broken]" (James 4:6; I Pet. 5:5).

Brokenness is not a one-time event. It leads to a lifestyle of honesty before God and man. Walking in brokenness keeps one in continuous revival. Roy Hession clarifies this: "Being broken is both God's work and ours. He brings His pressure to bear, but we have to make the choice. . . . All day long the choice will be before us in a thousand ways."[16] Since brokenness is the way into blessing, believers must live in brokenness before God and man.

Roy Hession sums up the matter well: "To be broken is the beginning of revival. It is painful, it is humiliating, but it is the only way."[17] But it is the way into blessing!

Summary of the Phases of Revival:

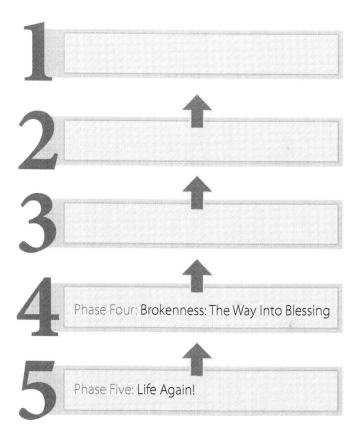

1.

2.

3.

4. Phase Four: Brokenness: The Way Into Blessing

5. Phase Five: Life Again!

The REVIEWAL
JOURNEY

The REVIVAL
JOURNEY

QUESTION FOR
THOUGHT:
Since brokenness
is the way into the
blessing of life again,
what brings people to
genuine brokenness?

Chapter Three

GOD HAS COME!

> Phase Three

*B*ut, Duncan, you can't possibly go! You're booked to speak at the closing meeting. The people will be disappointed."

It was Easter Monday, 1952. Duncan [Campbell] had just given an address . . . when he was suddenly arrested by a conviction that he should leave at once and go to Berneray, a small island off the coast of Harris with a population of about 400 people. Sitting in the pulpit, he tried to fight off the insistent urge, but the urgency only increased.

Eventually turning to the chairman, he said, "I must leave the Convention and go to Harris immediately." Objections were valid enough . . . but Duncan was unrelenting. "I'm sorry; I must obey the promptings of the Spirit and go at once."

He left the pulpit to pack his case and the following morning flew from Belfast to Scotland. On Thursday morning he reached Harris and took the ferry to Berneray. He had never been there before and knew no one on the island. The first person he met was a sixteen-year-old boy. "Could you direct me to the manse, please?"

"The manse is vacant," the lad replied. "We have no minister just now. The men . . . take the services," he said, and pointing to a house on the hill, added, "One lives up there."

Duncan glanced from the hill to his suitcase, and then back to the boy. "Could you please go and tell him that Mr. Campbell has arrived on the island. If he asks what Mr. Campbell, tell him it's the minister who was in Lewis."

Ten minutes later the boy came back to say that [Hector McKennon] was expecting him, accommodations had been arranged, and a service already intimated for nine o'clock that night! God had gone before.

Three days earlier when Duncan was in the pulpit at Bangor, this man had been praying in the barn. He had been there most of the day. God had given him a promise: "I will be as the dew unto Israel," which he had laid hold of in faith, assured that revival was going to sweep the island.

More than that, he was confident that God would send Duncan Campbell. His wife could hear him in the barn:

"Lord, I don't know where he is, but You know and with
You all things are possible. You send him to the island."
So convinced was he that God would bring him in three
days time that he made the necessary arrangements for a
mission [meeting].

The first few services were uninspiring. Duncan felt tired
and spiritually out of breath, but [Hector McKennon]
adamantly affirmed that revival was at hand.

One evening as they were preparing to leave the church,
the old man suddenly took his hat off, pointing excitedly
in the direction of the congregation which had just left
the service. "Mr. Campbell, see what's happening! He
has come! He has come!" The Spirit of God had fallen
upon the people as they moved down towards the main
road, and in a few minutes they were so gripped with the
subduing presence of God that no one could move any
further. Amid sighs and groans from sin-burdened souls,
prayer ascended to God on the hillside. The entire island
was shaken into a new awareness of God as many lives
were saved and transformed during the following days. In
this movement . . . the results were . . . deep and abiding.[1]

Hector McKennon was burdened about the condition of
the church on the little island of Berneray south of Harris,
which is the southern part of the island of Lewis. Undoubtedly,
the news of the Lewis Awakening had stirred his heart to seek
God. He spent the day in prayer and fasting, whereupon the
Spirit bore witness with his spirit, convincing him of the

words of Hosea 14:5, "I will be as the dew unto Israel." "About 10:00 that evening, he was possessed of the conviction that God had heard his cry."[2] After the first few services in which about 80 people attended, which is considerable since the island population was only about 400 people, God came down. In Duncan Campbell's account, he says, "Soon the whole island was in the grip of a mighty movement

Since God promises to pour out His Spirit in the church age, each generation must trust God for the outpouring.

of the Spirit, bringing deep conviction of sin and hunger for God . . . Perhaps the most outstanding feature was the awe-inspiring sense of the presence of God that came over the whole island."[3]

In this glorious account, when Hector McKennon declared, "He has come! He has come!" what did he mean? When Duncan Campbell stated, "Perhaps the most outstanding feature was the awe-inspiring sense of the presence of God that came over the whole island," to what was he referring?

Acts 2:16–17 explains, "But this is that which was spoken by the prophet Joel; And it shall come to pass in the last days, saith God, I will pour out of my Spirit upon all flesh." Since God promises to pour out His Spirit in the church age, each generation must trust God for the outpouring. However, several perplexing questions arise out of this passage. What is the outpouring of the Spirit? Is the outpouring of the Spirit for today? How is the outpouring of the Spirit accessed? These questions can and must be answered from the Word of God.

WHAT IS THE OUTPOURING OF THE SPIRIT?

As in the study of revival or "life again" in Chapter One, there are three defining issues that form a full conception of the outpouring of the Spirit.

The Defining Essence of the Outpouring of the Spirit Is the Manifestation of the Presence of God

Christ sent the Spirit on the Day of Pentecost. The Spirit has not been sent back. The outpouring of the Spirit therefore is not a matter of Christ resending the Spirit. Rather it is a matter of manifesting the sent Spirit. The Holy Spirit can withdraw the manifestation of His presence. The Holy Spirit can "hide God's face." Seeking the outpouring of the Spirit is therefore seeking the manifestation of God's presence.

Although there are many verses that speak of the outpouring of the Spirit,[4] the key defining verse is Ezekiel 39:29 because it not only mentions the outpouring of the Spirit, it gives the defining sense: "Neither will I hide my face any more from them: for I have poured out my Spirit upon the house of Israel, saith the Lord God." The word *face* [*paniym*] is often translated "presence." Ezekiel 39:29 defines *poured out my Spirit* with the phrase "Neither will I hide my face [presence] any more." In other words, the outpouring of God's Spirit is the manifestation of God's presence.

Similarly in Isaiah 64:1–3, the phrase "that thou wouldest come down," which parallels God pouring out His Spirit, is defined three times as "at thy presence." Isaiah uses the imagery of God coming down, while Ezekiel uses the imagery of God pouring out His Spirit. However both imageries are defined as the manifest presence of God.

Besides Ezekiel 39:29, the terminology of God pouring out His Spirit is used explicitly in Isaiah 44:3; Joel 2:28–29; and Zechariah 12:10. Also, the terminology of the Spirit being poured out is used in Isaiah 32:15. Implicitly, wisdom personified says in Proverbs 1:23, "I will pour out of my spirit." Isaiah 45:8 says, "Let the skies pour down righteousness," and Malachi 3:10 speaks of God opening the windows of heaven to "pour you out a blessing." Similar to "pouring out" is the "rain" imagery used in a spiritual sense in Psalm 72:6; Ezekiel 34:26 ("showers of blessing"); Hosea 6:3; 10:12 ("rain righteousness"); and Zechariah 10:1. "Water" is used in a spiritual sense in Psalm 107:33, 35; Isaiah 35:6–7 ("streams in the desert"); 41:18; 43:19–20; 49:10; Ezekiel 36:25; Hosea 14:5 ("dew"); and Zechariah 13:1 ("fountain").

Regarding God's presence being manifested, the terminology of God causing His "face" [presence] to shine on His people is used in Numbers 6:25; Psalm 31:16; 67:1; 80:3, 7, 19; 119:135; and Daniel 9:17 in Daniel's great revival prayer. The concept of a visitation from God is used in Jeremiah 29:10. The imagery of God breathing on His people is used in Ezekiel 37:9. Other images and concepts used in the Old Testament include God looking favorably on His people, God turning His countenance toward His people, God shining His light on His people, the glory of the Lord appearing to His people, God being with or among His people, and so forth. Although there are many other references addressing other aspects of revival, the citations listed here speak strictly of God's divine moving. In some way or other, they speak of the manifestation of the presence of God.

The New Testament incorporates the terminology of the outpouring of the Spirit explicitly in Acts 2:17–18; 2:33 ("shed forth" translates from the same word *ekcheo* as "pour out"); and 10:45. Implicitly, the imagery of the Holy Spirit "falling" on people is used in Acts 8:16; 10:44; and 11:15. Also, the imagery of the Spirit "coming" on people is used in Acts 1:8 and 19:6.

God's manifest presence is needed for genuine revival to take place. Second Chronicles 7:14 says, "Seek my face." Again *face* is literally "presence." Seeking revival is seeking God. It is not seeking the sensational but rather seeking God Himself. Seeking the outpouring of the Spirit in revival is simply seeking the manifest presence of God.

Spiritual, Not Physical

This manifest presence of God is spiritual, not physical. But it is just as real as if it were physical. For example on a personal note, God poured out His Spirit on a church I was with in Ireland during a church camp in the year 2000. The camp schedule included two services a day. Then under the Spirit's leading we held after-meetings, which

> *When God pours out His Spirit, sometimes it is immediately powerful like waves crashing over the rocks ... However, sometimes it is increasingly powerful as in the rising of the tide.*

were simply meetings that followed after the main meetings. Interestingly, the meetings after the meetings lasted longer than the meetings. O what a meeting with God night after night! One young lady who was there told me five years later that it was as if Jesus was personally present in those meetings. She said that if Jesus had appeared physically, He would have been no more real than He already was spiritually.

R. B. Jones relates the following from the Welsh Revival of 1904–1905:

> This all-pervading sense of the presence of God, even among the children, may perhaps be further illustrated by a story from Rhos. Someone overheard one little child ask another, "Do you know what has happened at Rhos?" "No, I don't, except that Sunday comes every day now." "Don't you know?" "No, I don't." "Why, Jesus Christ has come to live in Rhos now!"[5]

The reality of Jesus was spiritual, not physical, but it was obviously just as real as if it was physical—even to children.

Powerful, But Difficult to Describe

The manifest presence of God is also powerful but quite difficult to describe. How does someone describe the invisible? The only thing that can be described is man's response to God's spiritual presence, like people falling to their knees or crying out for mercy. Some get derailed by focusing on man's response, which often varies, rather than on the real issue of God's manifest presence. Again the key is to seek God's reviving presence—not a set of human responses that took place in a given revival scene.

When God pours out His Spirit, sometimes it is immediately powerful like waves crashing over the rocks. This was the case in the opening illustration of the chapter.

However, sometimes it is increasingly powerful as in the rising of the tide. In both cases the water goes over the rocks. The "rising-tide" style is less dramatic because of its more gradual nature, but it is nonetheless just as real.

Again on a personal note, I believe this "rising-tide" style of the outpouring of the Spirit occurred in the church my father pastored in the early 1980s. The church was primarily a "white-collar" church located in some fairly wealthy suburbs on Chicago's west side. Yet from the years 1980–1985, the church grew from about 450 to 1000. Evangelism grew in numbers and in power. People were saved, discipled, and assimilated into the church. Families were salvaged. God was mightily at work. Although I was in college during much of this time period, I remember that when I was home, I did not want to miss a church service. I did not realize it at the time, but this "draw" was the presence of God. The growth, both spiritually and numerically, during this time cannot be humanly explained. The rising of the tide of God's blessing had truly "covered the rocks." The only explanation is a season of refreshing from the presence of the Lord.

In summary, the outpouring of the Spirit is the spiritual, powerful manifestation of the presence of God. Duncan Campbell described this revival presence as a people being "saturated with God."[6] Before noting the next defining issue, a few examples from history will further illustrate the essence of the outpouring of the Spirit being the spiritual, powerful manifestation of God's presence.

The following is an account from the Cambuslang Revival with George Whitefield:

Mr. Whitefield's sermons on Saturday, Sabbath, and Monday were attended with much power, particularly that on Sabbath night about ten o'clock and that on Monday; several were crying out, and a very great but decent weeping and mourning was observable through the auditory.

On Sabbath evening, while he was serving some tables, he appeared to be so filled with the love of God as to be in a kind of ecstasy [sic], and he communicated with much of that blessed frame.

There was a good deal of outward decency and regularity observable at the tables. . . . But the thing most remarkable was the spiritual glory of this solemnity—I mean the *gracious and sensible presence of God*. . . . Many of God's dear children have declared that it was a precious time to their souls . . . some there were who wished, had it been the will of God, to be removed while waiting on God in these ordinances, without returning again to the world or their friends, and so to be with Christ in heaven [emphasis added].[7]

David Matthews, who was converted during the 1904 Welsh Revival, provides an account of the powerful presence of God:

When I left the heavenly atmosphere of the church for home, I discovered that it was five in the morning! I had been in the house of God for ten hours—they passed like ten minutes! Pushing through a throng that made progress slow, I discovered on the outside of the church that there were hundreds of people patiently standing—waiting in the chilly November air. They had been there all night, hoping somehow, sometime, for an opportunity to get inside God's house. Outside . . . one became instinctively conscious of a beautiful silence prevailing all around. *A presence, invisible but very real, pervaded the atmosphere. The air seemed electrified* [emphasis added].[8]

R. B. Jones, who was one of the preachers used of God in the north of Wales, wrote the following of the 1904–1905 Welsh Revival:

> *An atmosphere that is charged with the presence of God makes it as conducive as possible for backslidden saints to be restored to spiritual life and for sinners to receive eternal life without violating their will.*

The essential work of a Revival may well be the despair of any pen. The sensational provides "copy" for the journalist, but the more vital things are of little interest to him. A better service than the mere recital of incidents is, the present writer thinks, possible. If one were asked to describe in a word the outstanding feature of those days, one would unhesitatingly reply that it was *the universal, inescapable sense of the presence of God* [emphasis original].[9]

Again on a personal note, I had the opportunity in the summer of 2000 to go to the Island of Lewis and study the Lewis Revival of 1949–1953. While there, God in His providence allowed me to speak with a man who is mentioned in Duncan Campbell's biography as an intercessor. He told me with emphasis that during the revival the presence of God was so real you could almost reach out and touch it. As he spoke the words, he gestured with his hand several times. It was apparent that he was vividly remembering the reality of God's presence.

After a moving of the Spirit in revival at a church, the assistant pastor testified, "If you would have asked me two weeks ago what revival was, I could not have told you." Then with tears rolling down his cheeks he continued, "But I can tell you now—it's Jesus!" The essence of the outpouring of the Spirit is the spiritual, powerful manifestation of the presence of God.

The Defining Evidence of the Outpouring of the Spirit Is a Consciousness of the Presence of God

Duncan Campbell described the outpouring as that which produces "a consciousness of God." When people are arrested by a consciousness of God, they come to recognize a consciousness of sin—even sin of which they were formerly unaware. For many this further leads to a consciousness of the hope of deliverance. An atmosphere that is charged with the presence of God makes it as conducive as possible for backslidden saints to be restored to spiritual life and for sinners to receive eternal life without violating their will. The reason for this is that when God rends the heavens and comes down, He is banishing the powers of the air. The power of evil spirits is dispelled, and the power of the Holy Spirit is displayed. Therefore all the strongholds of deception in the thinking of people crumble. Without these hindrances, the Word of God has free course and is glorified or given weight by the Spirit. When truth is then preached in this atmosphere of God's manifest presence, it has the impact of its full weight. And an atmosphere pervaded by the Spirit is an atmosphere conducive to repentance and faith.

The totality of this picture is "greater works" (John 14:12). Jesus promised, "He that believeth on me . . . greater works than these shall he do; because I go unto my Father . . . and he shall give you . . . the Spirit of truth" (John 14:12–17). Christ's exaltation to the throne of His Father gave Him the authority to banish the powers of darkness, and the sending of the Spirit provided Him the means to manifest His glorified presence. When Christ dispels the spirits of deception and displays the Spirit of truth, this combination produces an atmosphere where conviction of truth is amazingly strong.

When Isaiah "saw also the Lord," he cried, "Woe is me! For I am undone." But God provided "a live coal" to touch him and pronounced, "Thy sin is purged" (Isa. 6:1–7). When Isaiah was aware of the presence of God, he was also immediately aware of the presence of his sin. So it is and must be when God manifests His presence. All the sin people rationalize away or have become desensitized to is seen for what it is when God's holy presence is felt. This accurate perspective produces the cry "Woe is me!"

No wonder Isaiah 64:1–2 speaks of God's coming down for the purpose "that the nations may tremble at thy presence."

Often when people in Scripture were confronted with God's presence, they fell on their faces to the ground. It should not be surprising when accounts in revival history provide similar details. For example, in a powerful moving of the Spirit in 2006 among a group of young people, they got down on the floor without any human leadership urging them to do so. One young lady later told her mother that it did not seem right for them to stay in their seats. This is not strange. It is simply the evidence of the outpouring of the Spirit.

After Peter declared that the events of the Day of Pentecost were the results of the outpouring of the Spirit and then preached in an atmosphere charged with the presence of God, the hearers, "pricked in their heart," responded with this heart cry: "Men and brethren, what shall we do?" (Acts 2:37). In Acts 2 there were 3,000 conversions. But in Acts 7 in a similar account, Stephen was stoned. For the religious seekers in Jerusalem in Acts 2, the awareness of sin produced a cry for deliverance. For the religious leaders who were hardened in their unbelief in Acts 7, the awareness of sin produced an attempt to silence the truth. This is why some use the phrase "revival or riot." When God pours out His Spirit, the presence of Jesus is manifested powerfully. To some He is the fragrance of life unto life, and to others He is the fragrance of death unto death (II Cor. 2:15–16). The point is the awareness of God produces an awareness of sin. In other words, the consciousness of God produces a conviction of sin.

If the essence of the outpouring of the Spirit is the manifestation of the presence of God, the evidence is a consciousness of the presence of God. This leads to conviction of sin and, for many, ultimately to deliverance through Christ.

After visiting the Welsh Revival of 1904–1905, G. Campbell Morgan said, "God has given Wales in these days a new conviction and consciousness of Himself that is the profound thing, the underlying truth."[10] It is this reality that is needed for a reviving and awakening work.

Failte don Eilean Sgiathanach—Welcome to the Isle of Skye. A present-day traveler crossing on the ferry to "the Misty Isle" from Kyle of Lochalsh would be greeted with these words on a large banner. But when Duncan [Campbell] crossed over in 1924 to commence mission-work, he was given the cold shoulder. Some unfortunate circumstance prior to his arrival had given the people a wrong impression of evangelistic work. Only a few faithful supporters, converts of previous missions, attended. Visiting produced no positive response; sometimes there was open antagonism. A woman slammed the door in his face, shouting: "Clear out the village. Clear out, you servants of the devil!"—an expression reckoned to be the worst insult you can throw at a religious person in the Highlands.

"Have faith in God" is the motto of the [Faith] Mission. Faith and prayer can remove mountains. One evening, faith to continue and confidently expect God to work was given when singing the hymn:

High are the cities that dare our assault;
Strong are the barriers that call us to halt.
March we on fearless and down they must fall;
Vanquished by faith in Him far above all.

Duncan gave himself to prayer, often walking the roads at night asking God to intervene. In the village were three young women who also knew how to pray. Leaving the meeting one night, one of them said: "God is going to work in this place; souls will be saved, but we must fight the battle on our knees."

They went home to pray. Duncan also prayed all night in a barn. After midnight one of the girls was assured that prayer would be answered and ran to the home of another with the message: "God has come! God has come! He is going to work! But we must pray right through." They continued until six in the morning.

> *God's people must recognize that there is a difference between a man preaching as a Spirit-filled man and a Spirit-filled man preaching in an atmosphere saturated with the presence of God.*

Next night the power of God fell upon the meeting. Souls groaned under the convicting power of the Spirit of God. . . .Attendance increased. The presence of God was felt through the entire community. Whole families were brought to Christ.[11]

Both the essence and the evidence of the outpouring are expressed in the words "God has come! God has come!" and "Souls groaned under the convicting power of the Spirit of God." A consciousness of God makes men conscious of their sin.

The following is another glorious account from the Lewis Awakening in December of 1949:

The service closed in a tense silence, and the building emptied. As he came down from the pulpit, a young deacon raised his hand and moving it in a circle above his head, whispered: "Mr. Campbell, God is hovering over. He is going to break through. I can hear already the rumbling of heaven's chariot wheels."

Just then the door opened, and an elder beckoned: "Come and see what's happening!" The entire congregation was lingering outside, reluctant to disperse; others had joined them, *drawn from their homes by an irresistible power* they had not experienced before. There were looks of deep distress on many faces.

Suddenly a cry pierced the silence; a young man who had remained in the church, burdened to the point of agony for his fellow-men, was pouring out his desire in prayer. . .The congregation swept back into the church. *The awful presence of God brought a wave of conviction of sin* that caused even mature Christians to feel their sinfulness, bringing groans of distress and prayers of repentance from the unconverted. Strong men were bowed under the weight of sin, and cries for mercy were mingled with shouts of joy from others who passed into life [emphasis added].[12]

The defining essence and evidence of the outpouring of the Spirit is portrayed in the following account by R. B. Jones from the Welsh Revival of 1904–1905:

A sense of the Lord's presence was everywhere. It pervaded, nay, it created the spiritual atmosphere. It mattered not where one went, the consciousness of the reality and nearness of God followed. Felt, of course, in the Revival gatherings, it was by no means confined to them; it was also felt in the homes, on the streets, in the mines and factories, in the schools, yea, and even in the theatres and drinking saloons. The strange result was that wherever people gathered became a place of awe, and places of amusement and carousal were practically emptied. Many were the instances of men entering public-houses, ordering drinks, and then turning on their heels leaving them on the counters untouched. The sense of the Lord's presence was such as practically to paralyze the arm that would raise the cup to the lips. Football teams and the like were disbanded; their members finding greater joy in testimony to the Lord's grace than in games. The pit-bottoms and galleries became places of praise and prayer, where the miners gathered to worship ere they dispersed to their several stalls [emphasis added].[13]

> The outpouring of the Spirit *focuses on God's divine moving, which in turn leads to* revival *that focuses on man's received blessing.*

One biographer states the point well when he describes revival in the time of Whitefield: "This new awareness of God brought about—as ever it must—a new awareness of sin and an earnest repentance." [14] As sin is confessed among the saints or as the lost turn to Christ, the same awareness of God's presence that produced conviction of sin will then produce great joy in the Lord. When people truly bend and break and experience the cleansing power of the blood, the love of God becomes overwhelming. As there once was an awareness of sin, there will be an awareness of God's love. This awareness of God's love produces joy. In fact, if there are those who are truly walking in revival reality at the time of an outpouring, their response will be joy instead of conviction. One pastor during the 1859 Revival of Ulster testified, "While the righteous exhibited joy, the ungodly quailed with fear, and on every face could be read the signs of either one or other of those conflicting emotions."[15]

The combination of the *essence* of the outpouring of the Spirit being the manifestation of the presence of God and the *evidence* being the consciousness of that presence producing a conviction of sin reveals the vital importance of the outpouring of the Spirit. God's people must recognize that there is a difference between a man preaching as a Spirit-filled man and a Spirit-filled man preaching in an atmosphere saturated with the presence of God. In the first instance, rivers of living water flow and those who came to drink receive a blessing (while everyone else remains largely un-helped). In the latter instance, those who did not come to receive a blessing may also receive a blessing by responding rightly to the arresting confrontation of God's presence. Therefore more than any other spiritual dynamic, the outpouring of the Spirit causes people to take their focus off of man as they come face to face with God. This provides the greatest opportunity for God to receive the greatest glory.

The Defining Extent of the Outpouring of the Spirit Is the Realm of the Manifestation of the Presence of God

Broadly, the extent of the outpouring of the Spirit may be individual or corporate. Specifically, however, several levels of extent may be delineated. These levels of extent parallel the levels discussed in Chapter One. First, the outpouring of the Spirit may take place on a personal level. For example, during a Cavalry charge in World War I, a young Duncan Campbell was rendered horseless and severely wounded. The prayer of Robert Murray McCheyne, which Campbell had often heard his father pray, came to his mind. "Lying on the horse's back, persuaded that he was dying, Duncan prayed it again in an agony of earnestness. Instantly, the power of God possessed him. Like a purging fire, the Holy Spirit swept through his personality, bringing cleansing and renewal until 'at that moment I felt pure as an angel.' The consciousness of God was so real that he concluded he was going straight to heaven."[16] This personal outpouring and subsequent personal revival led to the salvation of seven Canadian soldiers. Meeting with God in this way changed the course of Campbell's future as he saw firsthand the impact of the manifestation of God's presence.

The second level of extent is small group (e.g., Haystack Prayer Meeting, 1806), third is church-wide (e.g., Moravian Revival, 1727), fourth is community-wide (e.g., Jonathan Edwards, Northampton, 1735), fifth is regional (e.g., Lewis Awakening, 1949–1953), sixth is national (e.g., 1857–1858 Revival in America), and seventh is international (e.g., Great Awakenings). Concerning the 1857–1858 Revival in America, revival historian J. Edwin Orr said, "A Divine influence seemed to pervade the land, and men's hearts were strangely warmed by a Power that was outpoured in unusual ways."[17] But whether the outpouring of the Spirit is personal or to a larger extent, the dynamic is the same.

When people respond rightly to the Spirit's convicting presence, revival follows. Revival is a restoration to spiritual life—life in the Spirit. God's presence *to* believers (the outpouring of the Spirit) leads to God's presence *through* believers (the filling of the Spirit). In his account of the early twentieth-century revivals, J. Edwin Orr states that "there were . . . innumerable accounts of the outpouring of the Spirit and the infilling of believers."[18] *The outpouring of the Spirit* focuses on God's divine moving, which in turn leads to *revival* that focuses on man's received blessing. Yet the word *revival* may be used broadly to include both God's divine moving and man's received blessing. Therefore in the broadest defining sense that combines the outpouring of the Spirit and the "life again" of life in the Spirit, *revival is the spiritual, powerful manifestation of the presence of God that leads the saints to brokenness and a restoration to spiritual life and that awakens the lost to a reception of eternal life.*

IS THE OUTPOURING OF THE SPIRIT FOR TODAY?

That the outpouring of the Spirit is definitely for the entire New Testament age is supported by three reasons.

The Precision of the Inspired Wording

When Peter stood up to declare to the crowd what was happening on the Day of Pentecost, he clarified, "But this is that which was spoken by the prophet Joel; And it shall come to pass in the last days, saith God, I will pour out of my Spirit upon all flesh." (Acts 2:16–17a). The quotation comes from Joel 2:28, which says, "And it shall come to pass afterward, that I will pour out my spirit upon all flesh." A careful observation of both quotations reveals that there is a significant change of wording in Peter's quotation from Joel. Joel said, "And it shall come to pass *afterward*, that I will pour out my spirit upon all flesh." But Peter said, "And it shall come to pass *in the last days, saith God*, I will pour out of my Spirit upon all flesh." Under inspiration Peter changed the wording from Joel's prophecy. He replaced the word *afterward* with the phrase "in the last days, saith God."

While there is some debate as to the time reference of "afterward," it is clear in the context of Joel 2 that it refers to a significantly later time period than what the previous verses in Joel 2 address. Yet regardless of the actual time reference of "afterward" in Joel 2, in Acts 2:17, inspiration applies it to the period known as "the last days." Therefore, without diminishing what may still be yet future according to Joel, Peter, under inspiration, revealed God's purpose ("saith God") for the present New Testament age ("in the last days"). Apparently "the last days" included the Day of Pentecost and, even more apparently, "the last days" include the New Testament age (II Tim. 3:1; Heb. 1:2). Peter did not say "in the last day" or even "a day in the last days," but rather "in the last days." He even underscored this time reference with the words *saith God*. Also, he specified that the outpouring of the Spirit was intended for "all flesh." Therefore, it is the will of God for every generation in the New Testament age to know the mighty outpouring of His Spirit.

What a blessed promise revealing the purpose of God, and, therefore, what a blessed foundation for faith! The Word of God declares, "And it shall come to pass in the last days, saith God, I will pour out of my Spirit upon all flesh: and your sons and your daughters shall prophesy, and your young men shall see visions, and your old men shall dream dreams: And on my servants and on my handmaidens I will pour out in those days of my Spirit; and they shall prophesy" (Acts 2:17–18). The outpouring of the Spirit is most certainly for today.

> *Without the manifestation of the presence of God, the work of God struggles along with little impact.*

The Precision of the Inspired Phrasing

Some understandingly object, arguing that the statements of Acts 2:19–20 obviously are not for today: "And I will show wonders in heaven above, and signs in the earth beneath; blood, and fire, and vapour of smoke: The sun shall be turned into darkness, and the moon into blood, before that great and notable day of the Lord come." However, verses 19–20 are grammatically linked to the last phrase of verse 20: "before that great and notable day of the Lord come." In fact, the wording of these verses nearly parallels the prophecy Jesus gave in the Olivet Discourse: "Immediately after the tribulation of those days shall the sun be darkened, and the moon shall not give her light, and the stars shall fall from heaven, and the powers of the heavens shall be shaken: And then shall appear the sign of the Son in heaven: and then shall all the tribes of the earth mourn, and they shall see the Son of man coming in the clouds of heaven with power and great glory." (Matt. 24:29–30; cf. Mark 13:24–26). The events describe what will take place just before Christ descends in His second coming. Therefore the events of verses 19–20 are Tribulational, and the events of verses 17–18 began on the Day of Pentecost and are for the period called "the last days."

Verses 17–18 describe the events surrounding the descent of the Spirit, and, therefore, the inauguration of what might be termed "Christ's present spiritual kingdom." Verses 19–20 describe the events surrounding the descent of the Son, and, therefore, the inauguration of Christ's coming physical kingdom. This side-by-side phrasing should not be surprising in light of the prophetical passages that parallel the first and second advents (e.g., Isa. 61:1–2). This is not double meaning in the same phrases but single meaning in back-to-back phrases. The Jewish error was that they missed the blessing of the first advent by seeing only the truth of the Second Advent. In the same way, the church must not miss the blessing that God intends for today by seeing only the truth that is to come.

It may be wondered why verses 19–20 were even included since they refer to a later time than verses 17–18. The answer lies in verse 21, which was the major point Peter was making in his sermon: "Whosoever shall call on the name of the Lord shall be saved."

The Precision of the Inspired Context

A third reason supporting the assertion that the outpouring of the Spirit is for today lies in the context following Acts 2:17–21. As Peter's sermon progresses, he states in Acts 2:32–33, "This Jesus hath God raised up, whereof we all are witnesses.

Therefore being by the right hand of God exalted, and having received of the Father *the promise of the Holy Ghost,* he hath shed forth [lit., poured out] this, which ye now see and hear." Then in Acts 2:39, he refers again to the promise of the Spirit: "For the *promise* is unto you, and to your children, *and to all that are afar off, even as many as the Lord our God shall call"* (Acts 2:39). The last phrase includes present-day believers.

Therefore the inspired wording in the context of Acts 2:17ff. clarifies that the outpouring of the Spirit is in fact for today.

How Is the Outpouring of the Spirit Accessed?

How was the outpouring of the Spirit recorded in Acts 2 accessed? The answer may be found in Acts 1:14: "These all continued with one accord in prayer and supplication." Ten days later, the prayer meetings were continuing as "they were all with one accord in one place"(Acts 2:1). Then God came! The manifestation of the living Savior through the outpouring of the Spirit revived the saints and awakened the lost.

For what were they praying? In the context of Acts 1, the last words of Jesus Christ promised the powerful ministry of the Holy Spirit (Acts 1:4–5, 8; cf. Luke 24:49). Contextually, it seems safe to conclude that the disciples were praying for the fulfillment of the promise of the Spirit. They sought the Lord by praying for the ministry of the Spirit, based on the promise Christ had given them. Simply put, they exercised faith. Through faith they obtained the promise (cf. Heb. 11:33).

Undoubtedly, the disciples knew that without the manifestation of the Spirit's presence and power, there was no hope. They knew that they had failed their Lord in His crisis hour. They knew that the flesh would not profit. They needed the Spirit.

The same is true for every generation of believers. Without the manifestation of the presence of God, the work of God struggles along with little impact. Even though there is the ministry of the Word, there is a lack of life without the ministry of the Spirit. "The seed is rotten [shrivels] under their clods" (Joel 1:17). This is a physical picture of a spiritual truth. Planted seed needs the life-giving rain. Likewise, the seed of the Word needs the water of the Spirit. The seed of the Word sprouts and blossoms through the life-giving rain of the Spirit. Therefore each generation must seek the Lord for seasons of refreshing from the presence of the Lord. It should be no surprise that the Scripture enjoins God's people to "seek his face [presence] continually" (I Chron. 16:11). To not seek the Lord's presence indicates ignorance, apathy, or even idolatry. God's presence is the only answer. But God's reviving presence is the answer!

The work which Adoniram Judson began in Burma (Myanmar) eventually made its way throughout parts of the country. In time the gospel saw great impact in the tribal regions, including the western mountains of Myanmar known as the Chin Hills. Baptist churches sprang up among the various Chin tribes. However, when the American Baptist Convention became liberal in the first half of the twentieth century, the liberalism eventually invaded the Baptist churches of the Chin State. By the 1970s, many claimed Christianity, but they were not born again. They were nominal Christians—Christians in name only but not truly born again.

Yet in the providence of God, some young men from the Hakha Chin tribe went to India to attend a Bible college and found admission in Berean Baptist Bible College, founded by Jacob Chelli. Hearing the true gospel, they were born again. Later, they returned to their people with the desire to point them to Jesus Christ. However, their efforts seemed futile. In 1981 some began to intercede for revival.[19] Over the years, undoubtedly, God was purging and teaching. Then in early 2004, with the conviction that in order for their people to be reached they needed a mighty moving of the Spirit, several evangelists led a group of about 300 believers to a mountain to fast and pray for three days and three nights. With burdened hearts, they interceded for their people, asking God to open their blind eyes through a mighty moving of the Holy Spirit. This prayer vigil was held on three different occasions. Others led a group of 100 to another mountain for prayer and fasting, also for three days and three nights. This occurred three times as well.[20]

Finally, through the Holy Spirit's leading, the evangelists called for a gospel service. God poured out His Spirit, and 8,000 people came. Saints were revived, and several thousand unsaved were awakened and trusted Christ. In this visitation from on high, 2,000–8,000 people came for over 400 consecutive nights of services. Prayer meetings began each day at 4:00 A.M. and lasted several hours. Presumably, the people then went to work. The day then concluded with services in the evening. Almost one-third of the population of Hakha, which is the capital city of the Chin State, was born again. Seven or eight liberal pastors were converted. A number of churches have been planted, missionaries have been sent out, and evangelism has gone forward in supernatural power.[21] This recent account is an example of God's plan for this age— for God to come!

Dean David Howell wrote to his Welsh countrymen at the end of 1902 before he died: "The chief need . . . is a spiritual revival through a special outpouring of the Holy Ghost."[22] The same is true today regardless of one's country. Since God promises to pour out His Spirit in the church age, each generation must trust God for the outpouring. Through faith each generation must obtain the promise of the outpouring of the Spirit. May all with a heart for revival cry out with the hymn writer who wrote the following words in a time of revival at the beginning of the twentieth century:

> O Breath of Life, come sweeping through us,
> Revive Thy Church with life and power;
> O Breath of Life, come, cleanse, renew us,
> And fit Thy Church to meet this hour.

Summary of the Phases of Revival:

Phase Three: God Has Come!

Phase Four: Brokenness: The Way Into Blessing

Phase Five: Life Again!

*The*REVIVAL JOURNEY

QUESTION FOR
THOUGHT:
Since the outpouring of
the Spirit produces an
atmosphere conducive
to brokenness, when
does God "come"
manifesting His
reviving presence? In
other words, is there
a solid foundation
for faith that if God's
reviving presence is
sought, He will in fact
be found?

Chapter Four

SEEKING GOD'S REVIVING PRESENCE

Phase Two

*I*n 2003 God granted real revival within a local church. It was manifested during a revival meeting. During the last half of the meeting, after-meetings were held. As the Spirit of God brought conviction, there was brokenness—deep brokenness over sin and unbelief. Then as the blood brought cleansing, people took by faith a clean heart. This has led to transformed living. A year later the assistant pastor said that undoubtedly there was a group of people who were truly changed—revived.

How did this season of refreshing begin? About one year earlier, after some severe trials in the church, the assistant pastor read A. W. Tozer's book The Pursuit of God. The Spirit of God ignited a fire in his heart. He gave the book to his father, who was the pastor of the church. The fire spread. They passed the book to others until nearly fifteen people were stirred. They began a "fellowship of the burning heart" and met on Saturday mornings to "pursue God." One year later God granted His reviving presence.

But many wonder, is revival really accessible? Some believe that it is good to pray, but that there is no real foundation to actually expect revival to come. They believe that revival may or may not come according to God's arbitrary will. Therefore they believe that revival is simply a sovereign act of God. Others tend to manipulate matters, attempting to imitate real revival. But between both extremes is a biblical answer to the question.

The Scripture includes several themes that are essentially the same theme regarding revival. In fact, the various terminologies are often used in the same contexts. Sometimes the terminology is that if God's people return to God, God will return to them. Often the terminology is used of God's people crying out to God, and God delivering them. This particular concept covers more than spiritual revival. But the terminology that is most prevalent is what might be labeled "the seek-find theme."

Is this seek-find theme an obscure matter in the Scripture, or is it emphasized as a firm foundation for those seeking revival? It should be remembered that *revival* means "life again!" Spiritually, revival is a restoration to spiritual life—the life of God and therefore life in the Spirit, whether individually or corporately. So seeking revival is seeking God.

The seek-find theme occurs in both the Old and the New Testaments. In the Old Testament are found two Hebrew words translated "seek." Their meanings, their frequency of usage, and their contexts are significant.

One word (*baqash*) means "to seek, require, or desire," with a major derivative meaning "petition." The "root basically connotes a person's earnest seeking of something or someone. . . . Its intention is that its object be found."[1] This is not a mere casual seeking but rather the earnest and intense: "I must find!" The other word (*darash*) means "to seek with care, inquire, or require."[2] Although very similar to the first word, this word is often used in a cognitive sense with the goal of finding knowledge. Both words are translated "enquire," meaning simply "to ask." Inherent in the concept of *seeking* is *asking*. Asking is an expression of dependence or faith. In fact, in Hebrews 11:6 the word *faith* is parallel to the phrase "seek him."

> *Since God emphasizes the promise that to those who seek Him, He will be found, believers must seek God's reviving presence.*

Together these two Hebrew words for seek occur at least 70 times in the context of spiritual seeking and finding.[3] These 70 occurrences span the major genres of law, narrative, poetry, and prophecy and can be organized into three categories. First, there are the contexts that state explicitly the word *seek* and the word *find*. Second, there are the contexts that state explicitly the word *seek* and state the concept of *find* with other terminology or by way of demonstration. This accounts for the majority of the usages. Third, there are the contexts that state explicitly the word *seek* and simply imply the concept of *find*. Furthermore, there are several New Testament parallel occurrences that reaffirm the Old Testament truth.

Without question the Word of God emphasizes the seek-find theme. Inherent in the wording is the condition of *seeking* and then the promise of *finding*. Focusing on this emphasis can be used of the Holy Spirit to cultivate faith in one's heart. Since God emphasizes the promise that to those who seek Him, He will be found, believers must seek God's reviving presence. Practically, how does God emphasize this promise? This study will note three ways.

THE WORD OF GOD DIRECTLY STATES THE PROMISE

In the Old Testament are found six passages that state the seek-find theme as a promise. These six "promise passages" become key passages because promises are foundational to exercising faith (Rom. 10:17). These six passages are found in law, narrative, and prophetical literature. Significantly, of the six key promise passages, four have the words *seek* and *find* stated explicitly. In the other two passages, *find* is stated with other terminology. Also of the six passages, two use both words for *seek* and a third passage does within the context. Since the key to faith is the object of faith, these six seek-find promises form a solid basis of dependence for revival.

Deuteronomy 4:29

"But if from thence thou shalt seek the Lord thy God, thou shalt find him, if thou seek him with all thy heart and with all thy soul."

The first seek-find promise is given in the Law. This is where many great themes begin. Both words for *seek* are found in this articulation. Also, the word *find* is stated explicitly. The phrase *from thence* in context refers to a backslidden condition. The essence of the promise is this: If from a backslidden condition you seek the Lord your God, you will find Him. This is a wonderful foundation for faith.

Deuteronomy 4:29 includes two key thoughts. First, there is the matter of seeking God Himself ("seek the Lord thy God"). Seeking revival is seeking God—it is seeking God's reviving presence. Second, the seeking must be wholehearted, not halfhearted ("seek him with all thy heart and with all thy soul"). This is not a casual "it would be nice" seeking. Rather this is an earnest "I must find" seeking. Often God allows delays to purge the heart from mixed motives or half-heartedness. For some if revival comes, that is nice; but if does not, they are still fine. This perspective indicates that they are satisfied with things other than God. This is not the whole heart. The whole heart finds its satisfaction in God alone. Obviously there are certain earthly cares for which people must take responsibility, but the whole heart sets its affection on God and will not be satisfied apart from the realized presence of Him. When there is a wholehearted seeking after God, the promise is sure: "Thou shalt find him." What a blessed foundation for faith!

I Chronicles 28:9

"And thou, Solomon my son, know thou the God of thy father, and serve him with a perfect heart and with a willing mind: for the Lord searcheth all hearts, and understandeth all the imaginations of the thoughts: if thou seek him, he will be found of thee: but if thou forsake him, he will cast thee off for ever."

The second seek-find promise is found in narrative literature. The word for *seek* is used early in the verse of the Lord who *searcheth* the hearts. Then both *seek* and *be found* are stated explicitly. Here, however, the promise is given to an individual as David is speaking to Solomon. This provides an exciting principle. Even if one's corporate group does not seek the Lord, one as an individual may seek God on his own with the expectation of finding Him. The promise could not be clearer: "If thou seek him, he will be found of thee."

II Chronicles 7:14

"If my people, which are called by my name, shall humble themselves, and pray, and seek my face, and turn from their wicked ways; then will I hear from heaven, and will forgive their sin, and will heal their land."

Further in the narrative, after David's words to Solomon in I Chronicles 28:9, one of the greatest revival promises in the whole of Scripture is found. Evidently, Solomon had taken David's admonition to heart. First, Solomon built the Temple (II Chron. 5:1). Then he had the Ark of the Covenant, the symbol of God's presence, brought into the Temple in the prescribed manner (5:2–10). As the Levites praised the Lord with music, "the glory of the Lord" then "filled the house of God" (5:11–14). In this great dedication service, Solomon preached (6:1–11) and then prayed (6:12–42). His prayer focused on the essence of the seek-find theme of Deuteronomy. When Solomon had finished praying, God sent down fire and consumed the offerings. Again "the glory of the Lord filled the house" (7:1). After a week-long celebration, God appeared to Solomon at night in response to his prayer (7:12–22). Second Chronicles 7:14 is the heart of God's answer to Solomon's prayer. God Himself is speaking in the first person. *Seek* is stated explicitly, and the concept of *find* is stated with other terminology. The word *face* in the phrase *seek my face* literally means "presence." This is clearly a matter of seeking God's reviving presence. When the conditions of seeking are met, the promise is definite: "then will I."

Some may query whether or not this promise applies to New Testament Christians since it was given to the nation of Israel. But notice the precision of inspiration in this great verse: "If my people, which are called by my name." Who are God's people called by His name today? *Christians*—therefore New Testament believers can solidly claim this promise.[4] This revival promise is another blessed foundation for faith.

II Chronicles 15:2

"And he went out to meet Asa, and said unto him, Hear ye me, Asa, and all Judah and Benjamin; The Lord is with you, while ye be with him; and if ye seek him, he will be found of you; but if ye forsake him, he will forsake you."

Eventually the narrative moves to the Judean King Asa. In this promise, one word for *seek* is used, but the other word is used twice in the same context (15:4, 15). *Seek* and *be found* are stated explicitly. The promise could not be stated more clearly: "if ye seek him, he will be found of you." Also, the parallel phrase in this verse teaches that this should be ongoing, not just a one-time matter: "The Lord is with you, while ye be with him." God desires His reviving presence to be continuous. In fact, Scripture commands God's people to be continuously seeking God's presence: "seek his face [presence] continually" (I Chron. 16:11) and "seek his face [presence] evermore" (Ps. 105:4). These commands must not be neglected. The people of God are responsible to seek the presence of God continuously.

In the context of this promise, Asa and the people of Judah "entered into a covenant to seek the Lord God of their fathers with all their heart and with all their soul" (15:12). Oh, that every true church in America and around the world would enter into a covenant to seek the Lord wholeheartedly, for God's promise is that *He will be found!* And the finding would transform the present generation of God's people and enable a glorious harvest of lost souls. In very fact, the world would not be the same.

In the context, Asa and Judah "sought him with their whole desire; and he was found of them" (15:15). God was true to His word—and He always will be. The impact for Judah affected the next twenty years (15:10; cf. 15:19).

Jeremiah 29:13

"And ye shall seek me, and find me, when ye shall search for me with all your heart."

The fifth promise is found in prophetical literature. Jeremiah sent an inspired letter to the captives in Babylon. This promise is the key to that letter. Both words for *seek* are used in the statement of the promise, one of which is translated *search*. *Find* is also stated explicitly. The emphasis again is seeking God "with all your heart." Daniel recognized this promise as a conditional promise and applied it by setting his face to seek the Lord "by prayer and supplications, with fasting, and sackcloth, and ashes" (Daniel 9:2–3). This is wholeheartedly seeking the Lord. Clearly Daniel did not believe this promise would inevitably happen, but that it must be accessed by faith.

This understanding is vital to experiencing God's presence today. Revival is not given as an arbitrary whim of God. Rather man is responsible to obtain the promises of God for revival. As the saints in the faith chapter of Hebrews 11 "through faith . . . obtained promises" (Heb. 11:33), so the saints of every generation must obtain the promises of God's reviving presence through faith. When the Spirit of God illumines and convinces of the promise of God, then God is revealing His purpose to His people. However, as in Daniel's case, the promise must still be obtained through faith. Like Daniel, the people of God must set their faces to seek the Lord wholeheartedly to fulfill His Word.

> Revival is not a sovereign act of God bestowed arbitrarily. Rather revival is a promised response. So the lack of revival is not God's responsibility; it is man's responsibility.

Hosea 10:12

"Sow to yourselves in righteousness, reap in mercy; break up your fallow ground: for it is time to seek the Lord, till he come and rain righteousness upon you."

The prophet Hosea under inspiration provides another one of the great revival promises. *Seek* is stated explicitly, while *find* is stated with other terminology. This promise contains a beautiful imagery: "Seek the Lord, till he come and rain righteousness upon you." An example of this is the revival in Riga, Latvia in 1905, which "was described as a downpour of spiritual rain."[5]

Some say that people may pray for revival, but that revival may or may not come because that is the sovereign choice of God. However, this thinking overlooks the fact that this sovereign God tells His people how He works in six promises all essentially stating the same truth: *If you seek Him, He will be found of you.* To say that He may or may not be found is unbelief in God's sure Word. No true Bible believer would say that if one seeks the Lord for salvation, He may or may not be found. Why then do people doubt God's promise of His reviving presence?

God's emphasis through His repeated promise reveals His purpose. Simply put, God's Word reveals His will. Therefore God desires to revive His people when they are in need of life again. In fact, God promises to revive those who seek Him. Six times the promise is made clear that to those who seek God, He will be found. All six promises refer to revival, not salvation. The foundation for faith to seek God's reviving presence with expectancy is absolutely sure. The matter is not uncertain. Contrariwise, the Word of God is repeatedly certain. Therefore there is no excuse. Revival is not a sovereign act of God bestowed arbitrarily. Rather revival is a promised response. So the lack of revival is not God's responsibility; it is man's responsibility. It is man's responsibility to wholeheartedly seek God's reviving presence. The fact that the Word of God directly states the promise that to those who seek Him, He will be found ought to stir God's people to seek God's reviving presence with their whole heart.

A classic example regards Jonathan Edwards's famous sermon "Sinners in the Hands of an Angry God," which he preached in Enfield, Connecticut, during the First Great Awakening. He was filling the pulpit there on a given Sunday because his own church was not far away in Northampton, Massachusetts. The presence of God became so powerful that the agonizing cries of conviction among the people nearly drowned out Edwards's voice.⁶ But this event did not just "happen." Some burdened souls had spent the night crying out to God to grant His reviving presence to Enfield, since it appeared that Enfield was being passed by in the blessing that much of that region of Connecticut was then receiving.

> The district apparently was as yet untouched by the Awakening and indeed so unconcerned whether it should be, that neighbouring Christians had given a considerable part of the previous night to prayer lest "while the divine showers were falling around them," Enfield would be passed by. Edwards took as his text Deuteronomy 32:35, "Their foot shall slide in due time," repeating a sermon which he had given in his own church shortly before on the subject, "Sinners in the Hands of an Angry God."⁷

THE WORD OF GOD AMPLY ILLUSTRATES THE PROMISE

All the Old Testament illustrations of the seek-find theme come from time periods of revival. This is the point of the seek-find promises. A brief survey of the illustrations will encourage faith.

The United Kingdom

Both King David and King Solomon led God's people to seek the Lord. This was a high point spiritually in the history of Israel. The seek-find theme was a part of David's bringing the Ark of the Covenant to Jerusalem (I Chron. 16:10–11; cf. Ps. 105:3–4). This is significant in light of the fact that the Ark symbolized God's presence. The seek-find theme is found in several psalms of David (Pss. 9:10; 22:26; 24:6; 27:8; 34:4, 10; 40:16; 69:32; 70:4) as well as in Psalm 119 (2, 10), although not specifically ascribed to David, and in a psalm of Asaph from David's time (Ps. 83:16). The seek-find theme is found in David's instructions to Solomon (I Chron. 22:19; 28:8–9). Also this great theme is found at the time when the Ark of the Covenant, the symbol of God's presence, was moved into the Temple. Solomon prayed in essence regarding the seek-find theme, and God responded in the great promise noted previously in II Chronicles 7:14. Finally, Solomon speaks of seeking the Lord in Proverbs 28:5.

The Judean Revivals

The seek-find theme occurs throughout the high points of the southern kingdom of Judah. Sometimes a Judean king led the people to seek God. Other times the threat of war caused the king to lead God's people to seek the Lord.

The seek-find theme is found in the life and leadership of kings Jehoshaphat (II Chron. 17:4; 19:3; 20:3–4; 22:9), Asa (II Chron. 14:3–4, 7; 15:2, 4, 12, 15), Uzziah (II Chron. 26:5), Hezekiah (II Chron. 31:21), and Josiah (II Chron. 34:3, 21, 26; II Kings 22:13, 18). The passages cited include glorious accounts of God's deliverance. It is interesting to note that the kings mentioned are the major kings of Judah—because they led the people of God in revival.

While some may be surprised when revival comes, the faith-filled intercessors are not.

The Return of the Remnant

Lastly, the seek-find theme occurs in reference to Daniel (Dan. 9:3) and Ezra (Ezra 6:21; 7:10; 8:21–23; cf. 8:31) regarding the return of the remnant to the land.

In this survey of the illustrations of the seek-find theme, the seeking included fasting in the case of Jehoshaphat, Daniel, and Ezra. Each account includes its own glorious details. The Word of God is replete with ample illustrations that when God's people humbly sought their God wholeheartedly, it was not in vain. Believers in every generation must take encouragement from this to also seek God's reviving presence.

Church history also abounds with illustrations. For example, in J. Edwin Orr's book *The Flaming Tongue,* an account chronicling early twentieth-century revivals in at least fifty-seven nations, Orr goes to great effort to point out the specific intercession for revival that preceded the revival blessing.[8] It is instructive that Orr's investigation and research documents this vital factor. Those who think that revivals just "happen" are obviously not involved in the faith-filled intercession. While some may be surprised when revival comes, the faith-filled intercessors are not. Every revival has some believer or believers somewhere expectantly seeking God's reviving presence.

For example on a personal note, I have read two biographies of Andrew Murray. Murray was a part of the Great Revival of 1860 in South Africa, which began in the church he pastored in Worcester. Murray's own father had a practice of reading from revival history every Friday night to his family. Then he would go to his study to pray for revival in South Africa.

While the biographies point out that Andrew Murray's father prayed thirty years for revival, they do not mention any specific intercession in connection with where the revival actually began.

However, when I made a trip to South Africa in 2001, in the providence of God I discovered another key factor regarding the intercession. While visiting the church in Worcester where Murray was pastor when the revival began, a caretaker informed me that the town had recently run some articles in its newspaper about the Great Revival of 1860. After obtaining copies of a two-part article, I discovered a brief but vital historical fact written by a contemporary of Murray: "For years before his arrival in Worcester, a humble group of intercessors had worn a small footpath to a hilltop looking out over the town from where they prayed for the people."[9]

This is another of God's many illustrations that to those who seek Him, He will surely be found. God's ample illustrations scripturally and historically ought to inspire God's people to seek God's reviving presence.

THE WORD OF GOD SPIRITUALLY APPLIES THE PROMISE

Besides the direct statements of the seek-find promise and the many illustrations, passages abound that simply urge God's people to seek the Lord. A brief survey of the usages in the Old Testament will then be followed by a focus on the New Testament usages of the word seek that are applied to the believer. The New Testament application of the seek-find theme challenges the believer to seek the Lord wholeheartedly.

The Prophets

Three of the promise passages also could be categorized as the preaching of a prophet (II Chron. 15:2; Jer. 29:13; Hos. 10:12). Beyond this, the need to seek the Lord is urged in other prophetical preaching (Isa. 8:19; 45:19; 55:1, 6; Jer. 50:4–5; Lam. 3:25; Hos. 3:5; 5:15; Amos 5:4, 6; Zeph. 2:3; Zech. 8:21–22; Mal. 3:1). Some of these passages could be applied to one's seeking the Lord in salvation, because whether the issue is salvation or revival, the seek-find principle is the same. Isaiah 55:6 is a classic example: "Seek ye the Lord while he may be found, call ye upon him while he is near."

The Apostles

In the great faith chapter of Hebrews 11, verse six begins by emphasizing the absolute necessity of faith for everything: "But without faith it is impossible to please him." Then it explains, "For he that cometh to God must believe that he is, and that he is a rewarder of them that diligently seek him." The foundation for faith could not be clearer—those who seek God, find Him! Also it is significant that in this verse *seek him* is parallel to *faith*. Seeking God is exercising faith.

Although the word *seek* is not used in James 4:8, the concept clearly is: "Draw nigh to God, and he will draw nigh to you." This is essentially the same as the six promises noted earlier in the Old Testament. But here the condition is given as a command. The context of James 4 is a revival context. In fact on a personal note, my father used to say that James 4:6–10 is the II Chronicles 7:14 of the New Testament. The command to "draw nigh to God" must be obeyed, because God's purpose is revealed in His promise, "and he will draw nigh to you."

The Lord Jesus Christ

In the Sermon on the Mount, Jesus speaks of seeking. He first mentions seeking God's kingdom and His righteousness (Matt. 6:33; cf. Luke 12:31). Then in Matthew 7:7–8, He takes up the seek-find theme: "Ask, and it shall be given you; seek, and ye shall find; knock, and it shall be opened unto you: For every one that asketh receiveth; and he that seeketh findeth; and to him that knocketh it shall be opened." *Ask, seek,* and *knock* are all parallel expressions. Then in verse eleven Jesus applies the seek-find theme broadly: "If ye then, being evil, know how to give good gifts unto your children, how much more shall your Father which is in heaven give good things to them that ask him?" The broad application is to "good things." However, in Luke 11:13, Jesus applies the seek-find theme specifically to the Holy Spirit. This then is the key New Testament seek-find passage.

Luke 11:9–10 says "And I say unto you, Ask, and it shall be given you; seek, and ye shall find; knock, and it shall be opened unto you. For every one that asketh receiveth; and he that seeketh findeth; and to him that knocketh it shall be opened." Again, the way one seeks is to "ask." Then Jesus narrows the application in verses 11–13: "If a son shall ask bread of any of you that is a father, will he give him a stone? Or if he ask a fish, will he for a fish give him a serpent? Or if he shall ask an egg, will he offer him a scorpion? If ye then, being evil, know how to give good gifts unto your children: how much more shall your heavenly Father give the Holy Spirit to them that ask him?"

Several key thoughts reveal the power of this promise. First, the grammar focuses on the quality or ministry of the Holy

Spirit. The definite article *the* is actually absent, even though in English the definite article is always inserted because it would sound strange without it. This shifts the emphasis from the person named to the quality of that person. Therefore this is not a matter of asking for the indwelling of the Spirit but rather asking for the quality of the Spirit—Holy Spiritness. This is essentially the ministry of the Spirit. This is not a matter of receiving a second blessing but rather a matter of accessing one's first blessing. Although this promise includes many aspects of the Spirit's ministry, it certainly includes God's reviving presence.

Second, the foundation for expectant faith could not be more solidly proclaimed—and that by Christ Himself: "*How much more* shall your heavenly Father give the Holy Spirit to them that ask him?" Third, the continuous nature of the present tense used in the verbs *give* and *ask* in verse thirteen indicates that this is an ongoing asking and receiving—not a one time, once-for-all matter. Fourth, since the context defines *seeking* as "asking" and the specific application is for the ministry of the Holy Spirit, Jesus provides a foundation of faith for intercession for revival—for seeking God's reviving presence. The Lord Himself literally promises *how much more shall your Father in heaven keep giving the ministry of the Holy Spirit to those who keep asking Him.* The disciples applied this repeatedly in the Book of Acts.

Although Jesus does not use the seek-find terminology in John 14:12, He does emphasize the concept: "Verily, verily, I say unto you, He that believeth on me [seeking], the works that I do shall he do also; and greater works than these shall he do; because I go unto my Father [finding]." Because Christ ascended to His enthroned position at the Father's right hand far above the Enemy with "all authority" (cf. Matt. 28:18; Eph. 1:19–21) and because He sent His Spirit to manifest His presence in this age (cf. John 14:16–18), He encourages His disciples to believe in Him for greater works. In John 14:13–14, Jesus explains how this belief is initially expressed: "And whatsoever ye shall *ask* in my name, that will I do, that the Father may be glorified in the Son. If ye shall *ask* any thing in my name, I will do it." The context is greater works. The expression of faith is asking. The promise is finding, for Jesus said, "I will do it." This passage provides another great foundation of faith for revival.

Some object to applying John 14:12 to revival on the basis that the commentators do not mention this application. However, is it not possible that they may be writing from their lack of experience? Men like Jonathan Goforth saw clearly the application of revival in John 14:12 and wrote about it. What is "greater" in the spiritual realm of the workings of God among the affairs of men than the binding of the strong man and the plundering of his house that occurs when God pours out His Spirit in revival?[10]

Again on a personal note, in January of 2001, I was preaching in a Spiritual Awakening Conference in Ireland. After preaching on "The Promise of the Spirit" the opening night, several preachers questioned me about revival. Finally, one said, "Have you ever seen what you are preaching about?" This was a fair question. Had he asked this question two years earlier, I would have been unsure how to answer. True, I had seen personal revivals and some one-service touches (which still are real). Also, on two different occasions at the same church in West Virginia, the meeting I was in was extended—once for three days and another time for an extra week and a half because of God's working among His people as well as a blessed harvest of souls. This truly was a time of glorious revival. In fact, it was the first sustained corporate revival I had ever eye-witnessed in my ministry. But in those days I did not have the understanding and therefore confidence regarding the seek-find reality in revival. So I would have been hesitant in my response to this preacher's question.

> *May every believer respond as the psalmist did in Psalm 27:8: "When thou saidst, Seek ye my face [presence]; my heart said unto thee, Thy face [presence], Lord, will I seek."*

But in 1999, God convinced me of the foundation of faith for revival which moved me from wishful thinking to convincement. Intercession began in my own life as well as with a group of friends. Although for me the intercession was often feeble, nevertheless, it was begun. More importantly, other intercessors who really knew how to pray joined in as well. Then in the summer of 2000, God poured out His Spirit on a church in Ireland where I was ministering, affecting the lives of many in the church even to the time of this writing. Also in the fall of 2000, God powerfully moved among a group of folk in the Philippines, where an evangelist friend and I were ministering.

So that night in 2001, when asked the question "Have you ever seen what you are preaching about?" I could honestly answer "Yes!" The next night the power of God fell on that meeting and continued throughout the conference. Several preachers have testified that God transformed their lives through that blessed season of refreshing. Since then from time to time I have seen the Lord grant His reviving presence corporately both in America and other countries. I am not just talking about "good meetings," although I am grateful for those. I am talking about a keen sense of the presence of God—deep conviction, transparent brokenness, and changed lives. While longing to see so much more, I mention this to the glory of God—God's promises are real.

CONCLUSION

Through direct statement, ample illustration, and spiritual application, God emphasizes the promise that to those who seek Him, He will be found. Therefore God's people must seek God's reviving presence—for most surely He will be found. If some unwittingly have mixed motives or incorrect thinking, God will work to straighten that out, for He is bound by His own promise to give the ministry of the Spirit to those who ask Him. May every believer respond as the psalmist did in Psalm 27:8: "When thou saidst, Seek ye my face [presence]; my heart said unto thee, Thy face [presence], Lord, will I seek."

In fact, as noted earlier the Scripture commands, "Seek his face [presence] continually" (I Chron. 16:11). God means for His people to obey this imperative. Seeking God's presence is to be a regular part of the lives of God's people. To not seek the presence of the Lord is to disobey this command. Furthermore, the context of this admonition provides clarity to the focus of the seeking: "Seek the Lord and his strength, seek his face continually." God's people are commanded to seek communion with God's person, the demonstration of His power, and the manifestation of His presence. This is seeking God's reviving presence.

Individually, believers must start seeking God's reviving presence by simply asking for the reviving presence of God. Awareness of need and convincement of God's promise to meet that need produces intensity of desire. Intensity of desire produces fervent prayer based on God's exceeding great and precious promises. Prayer based on God's specific promises is simply an expression of faith. It is God-dependence based on God's words. The first expression of faith regarding God's promises is simply asking. Believers must simply start asking for the reviving presence of God. Man's responsibility is always faith, and faith is not a work; it is dependence on the Worker.

Corporately, believers should meet together for the sole purpose of seeking God's reviving presence through the outpouring of the Holy Spirit. This is a revival prayer meeting. As God stirs this one and that one, there can be a joining together in a "heart-cry meeting" to cry out to God for deliverance from defeat and deadness. Jesus spoke of two's and three's joining to symphonize in prayer (Matt. 18:19–20). A "symphony of prayer" is simply a genuine looking to the Holy Spirit as the conductor, based on the score of the Word of God, to lead believers as instruments in a symphonizing of burden and faith in prayer.[11] The rise of the Second Great Awakening began as God's people joined in what was known as the "Concert of Prayer."[12]

An additional potential aspect of corporate seeking is the biblical concept of the Solemn Assembly, where spiritual leadership trusts God to lead God's people to corporate repentance and prayer for revival.[13]

The key to these practical aspects of the implementation of seeking is in obeying the Holy Spirit. It is not a matter of imitating the detail of a particular revival account. The point is that God's people must seek God's reviving presence. Revival prayer meetings, where the single aim is asking for the outpouring of the Spirit, are the responsibility of every generation. May intercessors arise with the single purpose of the prayer warriors of the 1859 Revival in Ulster: "It was a fellowship meeting of Christians met for the one great object of praying for an outpouring of the Holy Spirit upon ourselves and upon the surrounding country. This was the one great object and burden of our prayers. We held right to the one thing and did not run off to anything else."[14]

Summary of the Phases of Revival:

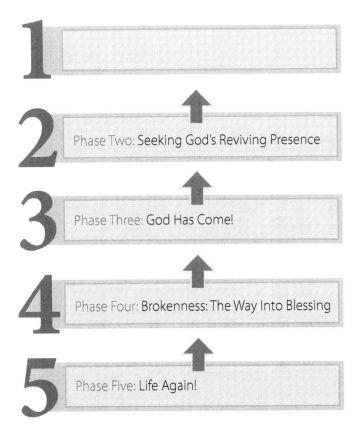

*The*REVIVAL JOURNEY

QUESTION FOR
THOUGHT:
Since God promises
to be found by those
who seek His reviving
presence, why and
when do people seek
God and especially
His reviving presence?

Chapter Five

THERE MUST BE MORE!

Revival journeys—whether individually or corporately—begin with the awakening that there must be more! This is a real awakening to need and to God's answer to that need. Jesus taught in John 14:20, "At that day ye shall know that I am in my Father, and ye in me, and I in you." Every believer needs to consider, "Have I awakened to the possibilities of 'that day'?" What are the possibilities of "that day"? The Scripture indicates two broad categories of awakening to need: personal revival and corporate revival. Both levels of awakening are taught by Jesus in John 14–16, demonstrated in Acts, and reinforced in the Epistles. The "something-more" longing arises from becoming aware of the stark contrast between the biblical presentation of normal Christianity and the lack of such reality in one's experience.

Personal Revival

Personally, I will never forget "that day" when by God's grace I started on my revival journey. Having heard much about real revival from my father, I had a desire for revival. But I had little understanding of what revival really was and how to access it. Then in the fall of 1991 at my father's urging, I began to read the two-volume biography of Hudson Taylor. In 1992 in the providence of God, I was also doing an inductive study of Galatians and Ephesians. The Spirit began to illuminate the word *grace* as "Spirit-enablement." The culmination of the reading and study came in early 1993 as God opened my eyes to the futility of the flesh and the necessity of the Spirit, the futility of flesh-dependence and the necessity of God-dependence, the futility of flesh-activity and the necessity of Spirit-enablement. For me this was the dawning of a new day—"that day." Since then God has filled in and is continuing to fill in many more details. But it was the beginning of a revival pilgrimage that has not ceased.

> *The "something-more" longing arises from becoming aware of the stark contrast between the biblical presentation of normal Christianity and the lack of such reality in one's experience.*

Once while in a local church series of meetings, I preached a progression of truth on the Spirit-filled life. A young businessman took me out for coffee and, referring to the emphasis on the Spirit-filled life, said, "Isn't this the missing ingredient?" In other words, he was realizing *there must be more!*

More than once preachers and others have testified to me that the day came when they realized *there must be more!* One pastor went on to say that his church people were also beginning to realize that "there is something more!"

If the Bible seems dry; if Christ does not appear magnificent; if there is not a vibrant relationship with the Lord; if the world, the flesh, and the devil seem overwhelming; if there is regular defeat (especially in certain areas) surprised by victory rather than regular victory surprised by defeat; if the works of the flesh prevail instead of the fruit of the Spirit; if the heavens seem brass and there are few answers to prayer; if there is little or no fruit in the realm of souls; if there is no persecution; if there is no demonstration of the Spirit and of power, then realize—*there must be more!*

By viewing the mountain peaks in the mountain range of the abundant "more" life, revival journeys may be launched.

The Victorious Promise of the Spirit: Life in the Spirit Declared

Jesus promised that the Father "shall give you another Comforter, that he may abide with you for ever; Even the Spirit of truth" (John 14:16–17). He further promised, "I will send him unto you" (John 16:7). How is this promise of the Spirit a promise of victory?

The Foundation for Victory by Faith

Jesus articulates the foundation for victorious living by faith when He says, "Ye in me, and I in you" (John 14:20). This beautifully describes a two-fold provision for believers.

New Position of Divine Authority

The first provision is the reality of "ye in me," which is the believer in Christ. Jesus also said, "Because I go to my Father" (John 14:12). Therefore the believer in Christ is with Christ at the throne of the Father. This position entitles the believer with delegated divine authority.

New Power of Divine Ability

The second provision is the reality of "I in you," which is Christ in the believer. When Jesus promised that the Spirit "shall be in you" (John 14:17), He immediately explained, "I will come to you" (John 14:18). The Spirit does not merely come in the stead of Christ; He brings Christ to live in the believer. This power endues the believer with imparted divine ability.

The Manifestations of Victory by Faith

Jesus emphasizes three major manifestations of victory through the Spirit. In so doing, He is portraying what life in the Spirit is like.

New Comprehension

First, life in the Spirit provides a vibrant illumination of the Scripture. "The Spirit of truth" (John 14:17; 15:26; 16:13) "will teach you all things" (John 14:26) and "guide you into all truth" (John 16:13). He takes that which is Christ's, who is at oneness with the Word (John 1:1, 14) and "shall show it unto you" (John 16:14; cf. v. 25). One pastor who experienced an awakening testified several months later that passages he had studied for years were coming alive—that it was as if "all things are become new."

Second, life in the Spirit also provides a vibrant exaltation of the Savior. Jesus promises that to the one who loves Him, "I will love him, and will manifest myself to him" (John 14:21). How does this manifestation of Christ take place? Jesus further promises that "the Spirit of truth ... shall testify of me" (John 15:26) and "shall glorify me" (John 16:14). Not only does the Spirit illuminate the Scripture—the inscribed Word—but He also exalts the Savior—the incarnate Word. Truly there is a mystery of oneness in these two aspects. When life in the Spirit dawns on the horizon of the believer's heart, God manifests Himself, and the Son rises in His full glory.

New Transformation

The new comprehension of the living Word opens the way for new transformation by that same living Word.

First, since life in the Spirit is a life of faith, there will be definite answers to prayer. Jesus promises in the context of authority, "And whatsoever ye shall ask in my name, that will I do ... If ye shall ask any thing in my name, I will do it" (John 14:13–14). Jesus promises in the context of abiding, "If ye abide in me, and my words abide in you, ye shall ask what ye will, and it shall be done unto you" (John 15:7). In the context of bearing fruit, Jesus promises "that whatsoever ye shall ask of the Father in my name, he may give it you" (John 15:16). In the context of "that day," Jesus promises, "Whatsoever ye shall ask the Father in my name, he will give it you. Hitherto have ye asked nothing in my name: ask, and ye shall receive" (John 16:23–24).

Second, life in the Spirit provides supernatural power in obedience. Faith accesses grace. Jesus promises, "If ye love

me, [you will] keep my commandments" (John 14:15)
because the Spirit will "abide with you" (John 14:16). Jesus
clarifies this promise further by stating, "If a man love me, he
will keep my words" (John 14:23).

Man is responsible to respond to the stirrings of the
Spirit. When he does, Jesus explains, "He that hath my
commandments, and keepeth them, he it is that loveth me"
(John 14:21). This is the key: love, trust, obey. Love for Christ
("he it is that loveth me") is expressed through dependence
on Christ ("He that hath [is having] my commandments"),
enabling obedience to Christ ("and keepeth them").

To love Christ is to choose Christ. To choose Christ is to
choose His words. To choose His words is to depend on His
words. To depend on His words is to be enabled by His Spirit.
To be enabled by His Spirit is to obey. The Spirit of Christ in
the believer is the power to obey. No wonder Jesus said, "Be
of good cheer; I have overcome the world" (John 16:33).

Third, life in the Spirit therefore evidences the fruit of the
Spirit. Jesus specifically emphasizes love (John 15:9–10, 12–
13, 17), joy (John 15:11; 16:20–22, 24), and peace (John
14:27; 16:33).

Fourth, life in the Spirit also produces the fruit of a
Christian—reproduction of believers. This is the picture of
the True Vine producing fruit through the abiding branches
(John 15:1–8, 16). As the believer abides in Christ through
God-dependence, Christ abides in the believer through
Spirit-enablement. When this is the case, "the same bringeth
forth much fruit." As the non-abiding life of self-dependence
is fruitless—"for without me ye can do nothing"—so the
abiding life of God-dependence for Spirit-enablement is

fruitful—for with Me you can do everything you ought to do.

New Persecution

One often overlooked part of the victorious promise of the Spirit is the persecution that comes with the blessing. In the context of life in the Spirit, Jesus indicates that "the world hateth you" and "will also persecute you" (John 15:18–21). Persecution involves various types of rejection and even the possibility of martyrdom (John 16:1–4). This is because the world hated—and still hates—Jesus (John 15:18).

> *As the non-abiding life of self-dependence is fruitless—"for without me ye can do nothing"—so the abiding life of God-dependence for Spirit-enablement is fruitful—for with Me you can do everything you ought to do.*

The more the life of Jesus is revealed through a believer, the greater the attraction is to some and the more repelling it is to others.

The Victorious Example of Acts: Life in the Spirit Demonstrated

Jesus instructed the disciples to "wait for the promise of the Father, which, saith he, ye have heard of me" (Acts 1:4). They had heard Him teach the victorious promise of the Spirit in Luke 11:13 and John 14–16. Then when the exalted Jesus received the promise of the Holy Spirit from the Father, He sent the Spirit, and the age of the Spirit was gloriously begun (Acts 2:33).

Concerning the foundation for victory by faith, the disciples in Acts realized their provision of divine authority over the powers of darkness (Acts 5:16; 8:6–7; 16:16–18; 19:11–20) as well as their provision of divine ability over the world and the flesh.

Concerning the manifestations of victory by faith, the disciples in Acts provide a thorough demonstration. Regarding new comprehension, Old Testament texts were often illuminated for preaching (Acts 2:14–36; 3:12–26; 4:8–12; 7:2–53; 8:32–35; 13:15–41, 46–47; 15:13–21; 23:5; 26:22–23; 28:25–28) and for personal discipleship as with Aquila and Priscilla instructing Apollos (Acts 18:24–26). Also, the exaltation of Christ to the hearts of the disciples was evidenced in their exaltation of Christ to others (Acts 2:22–24, 30–33, 36; 3:6, 13–16, 26; 4:10–12, 33; 5:30–31; 8:5, 35; 10:36–43; 13:30–39; 16:18; 17:3, 31; 18:28; 21:13; 26:23; 28:31).

Regarding new transformation, the disciples saw definite answers to prayer (Acts 1:14; cf. 2:1ff.; 4:24–31; 6:6–7; 9:40; 12:5–17; 13:2–3; 16:25–34; 28:8). They experienced power in obedience—both in the fruit of the Spirit (Acts 2:44–47 [love]; 5:41; 8:8, 39; 13:52; 15:3, 31; 16:34; 20:24 [joy]) as well as in the reproductive fruit of the Christian in souls (Acts 2, 4, 5, 6, 8, 10, 13, 14, 16, 17, 18, 19).

Many of the believers in Acts experienced the abundant life in every sense of the word.

Regarding new persecution, the disciples experienced Satan's hatred of the living Savior manifested through yielded believers (Acts 4:1–22; 5:17–41; 6:9–15; 7:54–8:4; 9:1–2, 23–25,29–30; 12:1–4; 13:50; 14:5–6,19; 16:19–24; 17:5–

9,13; 18:12–17; 19:23–41; 20:3; 21:27–39; 22:22–29; 23:9–10, 12–33; 24:22–27; 25:1–12; 27:1; 28:16, 30).

The Victorious Teaching of the Epistles: Life in the Spirit Explained

The Epistles largely expand what is taught by Christ in John 14–16 and what is demonstrated in Acts. In fact, "Acts provides the historical background necessary to understand the teaching of the Epistles that will follow."[1] In other words, the Epistles must be understood in the light of the book of Acts. The details of the Epistles regarding the victorious life of Christ accessed by faith through walking in the Spirit are much larger than the purpose of this chapter. Therefore only a summary will be provided.

Comprehensive Divine Provision

Regarding the believer in Christ providing the divine authority of an enthroned position, the Epistles incorporate "in Christ" or its equivalent phrases 216 times out of the 242 occurrences in the New Testament. This is a remarkable emphasis. Paul under inspiration explains the significance of this new position in Ephesians 1 by stating that Christ is seated "far above all principality, and power, and might, and dominion, and every name that is named" (Eph. 1:20–21) and that believers are seated "together in heavenly places in Christ Jesus" (Eph. 2:6). This "throne seat" is the provision of divine authority to counterattack and overrule the powers of darkness in the unseen realm where the real spiritual battle lies (Eph. 6). Many glorious biblical affirmations exemplify this position in Christ. One example is II Corinthians 2:14:

"Now thanks be unto God, which always causeth us to triumph in Christ."

Regarding Christ in the believer providing the divine ability of an indwelling person, again the scriptural references are numerous: "I live; yet not I, but Christ liveth in me . . . faith" (Gal. 2:20); "Christ in you, the hope of glory" (Col. 1:27); "Christ, who is our life" (Col. 3:4); "For to me to live is Christ" (Phil. 1:21). These words are life-giving foundations for faith. Christ in the believer is the provision of divine ability to counteract and overcome the world and the flesh in the physical realm of the "seen."

Basic Human Responsibility

The provision of life in the Spirit is to be accessed by faith. "But without faith it is impossible to please him" (Heb. 11:6). As the reception of the Spirit is by faith, so also is spiritual growth by faith (Gal. 3:2–3). "He therefore that ministereth [is supplying] to you the Spirit" does so by "faith" (Gal. 3:5).

In viewing the mountain peaks of the victorious promise of the Spirit, the victorious example of Acts, and the victorious teaching of the Epistles, many facts and promises tower above the valleys. With such a view of divine facts and promises, a right response is vital. As Evan Hopkins so aptly states, "Dare to face these promises and . . . claim them as a Scriptural experience."[2]

CORPORATE REVIVAL

Realizing "There must be more!" on the personal level is the beginning of the journey to personal revival. When personal revival is experienced, faith is strengthened. The believer learns what it is to be filled with the Spirit—and know it. This confidence is based on the sure words of God. This is not arrogance. It is simply taking God at His Word.

Then there lies the possibility of the Holy Spirit convincing the believer of "greater words" for "greater works." This truth is the primary burden of this book. Revived believers individually must realize that in the matter of corporate ministry impact—*there must be more!*

For example, Jonathan Goforth related his awakening to "greater works" in the following account:

> Upon returning to China in the fall of 1901, after having recuperated from the harrowing effects of the Boxer ordeal, I began to experience a growing dissatisfaction with the results of my work. In the early pioneer years I had buoyed myself with the assurance that a seed-time must always precede a harvest, and had, therefore, been content to persist in the apparently futile struggle. But now thirteen years had passed, and the harvest seemed, if anything, farther away than ever. I felt sure that there was something larger ahead of me, if I only had the vision to see what it was and the faith to grasp it. Constantly there would come back to me the words of the master: "Verily, verily, I say unto you, he that believeth on me, the works that I do shall he do also; and greater works than these shall he do . . ." And always there would sink deep the painful realization of how little right I had

Then there lies the possibility of the Holy Spirit convincing the believer of "greater words" for "greater works."

to make out that what I was doing from year to year was equivalent to the "greater works."

Restless, discontented, I was led to a more intensive study of the Scriptures. Every passage that had any bearing upon the price of, or the road to, the accession of power became life and breath to me. There were a number of books on Revival in my library. These I read over repeatedly. So much did it become an obsession with me that my wife began to fear that my mind would not stand it. Of great inspiration to me were the reports of the Welsh Revival of 1904 and 1905. Plainly, Revival was not a thing of the past. Slowly the realization began to dawn upon me that I had tapped a mine of infinite possibility.

Late in the fall of 1905 Eddy's little pamphlet, containing selections from "Finney's Autobiography and Revival Lectures," was sent to me by a friend in India. It was the final something which set me on fire. On the front page of this pamphlet there was a statement to the effect that a farmer might just as well pray for a temporal harvest without fulfilling the laws of nature as for Christians to expect a great ingathering of souls by simply asking for it and without bothering to fulfill the laws governing the spiritual harvest. "If Finney is right," I vowed, "then I'm going to find out what those laws are and obey them, no matter what it costs." Early in 1906, while on my way to take part in the intensive evangelistic work which our mission conducted yearly at the great idolatrous fair at Hsun Hsien, a brother missionary loaned me the full "Autobiography" of Finney. It is impossible for me to estimate all that that book meant to me. We missionaries read a portion of it daily while we carried on our work at the fair.

It was at this fair that I began to see evidence of the first stirrings in the people's hearts of the greater power. One day, while I was preaching on I Timothy 2:1–7, many seemed deeply touched. An evangelist behind me was heard to exclaim in an awed whisper, "Why, these people are being moved just as they were by Peter's sermon at Pentecost." That same evening, in one of our rented halls, I spoke to an audience that completely filled the building. My text was I Peter 2:24: "He bore our sins in His own body on the tree." Conviction seemed to be written on every face. Finally, when I called for decisions, the whole audience stood up as one man, crying, "We want to follow this Jesus Who died for us." I expected that one of the evangelists would be ready to take my place; but what was my surprise, when I turned around, to find the whole band, ten in number, standing there motionless, looking on in wonder. Leaving one to take charge of the meeting, the rest of us went into an inner room for prayer. For some minutes there was complete silence. All seemed too awed to say anything. At last one of the evangelists, his voice breaking, said: "Brethren, He for Whom we have prayed so long was here in the very deed tonight."[3]

This was the beginning of greater blessing in Goforth's ministry. But it all began when Goforth realized "there was something larger"—*there must be more!* Then when the Korean Revival of 1907 beamed brightly, Goforth went to see the wonderful works of God. He recalled:

The Korean movement was of incalculable significance in my life because it showed me at first-hand the boundless possibilities of the revival method. It is one thing to read about Revival in books. To witness its working with one's own eyes and to feel its atmosphere with one's own heart is a different thing altogether. Korea made me feel, as it did many others, that this was God's plan for setting the world aflame.[4]

Upon returning to China, Goforth travelled through Manchuria. As he did, he declared how the Spirit's fire was sweeping Korea. God so moved that Goforth was invited back to Manchuria to preach. The resulting season of refreshing in 1908 he recounts in his classic *By My Spirit*.[5]

Revival stirs faith for more revival. For example, accounts of the Welsh Revival of 1904–1905 circulated around the globe at that time. Many were stirred to pray for God to bless them also since God is not a respecter of persons. Among many others, the saints of Kassia Hills, India, began to pray. God poured out His Spirit on them in 1906. Word spread of this revival in India. The saints in Korea heard of God's blessing in India and prayed that God would pour out His Spirit on them as well. God heard and answered in 1907. As just noted, this fueled faith for the Manchurian Revival of 1908.

Also as mentioned in the previous chapter, Andrew Murray's father read a chapter from revival history to his family every Friday evening. Then he went to his study and behind closed doors cried out to God for a mighty outpouring of the Spirit in South Africa. Often Andrew Murray sat outside the door as a young boy and listened as his father wept and interceded for South Africa. It is no accident that

Andrew Murray became the human instrument used of God in the Great Revival of 1860. Murray's father understood the dynamic that revival stirs faith for more revival. By reading accounts of God's wonderful works in the past, he was stirred to cry out to God to bless in revival again.

As personal revival begets faith for corporate revival, so also corporate revival begets faith for more corporate revival. When faith is thus ignited, believers begin to realize the truth of these words of Jesus: "O fools, and slow of heart to believe all that the prophets have spoken" (Luke 24:25).

As personal revival begets faith for corporate revival, so also corporate revival begets faith for more corporate revival.

The promises of God providing a foundation of faith for revival are many. Some of the New Testament classics include the following: "Verily, verily, I say unto you, He that believeth on me, the works that I do shall he do also; and greater works than these shall he do; because I go unto my Father" (John 14:12); "And it shall come to pass in the last days, saith God, I will pour out of my Spirit upon all flesh" (Acts 2:17a); "And what is the exceeding greatness of his power to us-ward who believe, according to the working of his mighty power" (Ephesians 1:19); and "Now unto him that is able to do exceeding abundantly above all that we ask or think, according to the power that worketh in us" (Ephesians 3:20).

Sometimes people object to highlighting a verse like John 14:12 as a promise for revival, claiming that the commentaries do not interpret it that way. However, as noted in the previous chapter, it is possible that some commentators are interpreting such verses according to their lack of experience. Jesus connected greater works to His soon-to-be exalted and authoritative position with the Father (John 14:12b) and then His sending of the Spirit (John 14:16).

The reality of this is demonstrated in Acts and explained in the Epistles as highlighted in this chapter.

Regarding my personal journey on revival, God "blossomed" the faith that He had budded in my heart in 1992–1993. This blossoming continued over the next decade (and still continues). The Spirit keeps turning the diamond of revival truth and shines yet another facet of that truth into my heart.

Over the decade of the 1990s, I read much on the Spirit-filled life, which is the essence of personal revival. I noticed that many of the authors emphasized the importance of John 14–16. Also, I became intrigued with Acts 1–2. Through divine providence, in January 1999, I became insatiably thirsty to understand these two portions of Scripture. Yet for about two and a half months I felt like I was in the dark. I read these chapters repeatedly, but I knew that I had only a very surface understanding of them. Then sometime in March 1999, the Spirit began to shed light first on Acts 1–2 and then nearly simultaneously on John 14–16. For the first time in my life I began to experience the "inexhaustibleness" of the riches of the Word of God. It was a breathtaking time with God in His Word. For three months truth after truth was highlighted by the Spirit of truth. The promise of Acts 2:17 burned brightly as never before. No longer was revival something to be merely stirred about but in reality beyond one's grasp. For the first time the Spirit of Jesus convinced me of revival as God's desire and plan for this age. The foundation was being laid to trust God for corporate revival. Simultaneously, many details regarding personal revival crystallized as never before. The impact of this time period has fuelled my preaching ever since.

As noted in the previous chapter, intercession began for the outpouring of God's Spirit. Though at times the implementation of truth was feeble, God graciously led and blessed. Other streams converged in the providence of God. About one year later, God allowed me to eyewitness a sustained season of refreshing from His presence in a local church, which has been life-changing to many including me. Since then God has graciously granted several more "seasons," which prior to my revival journey were foreign. O to believe God for more of His desire to grant His reviving presence!

Then in 2006–2007, through more providential guidance, the Holy Spirit highlighted the tremendous truth of the believer's authority in Christ, especially Ephesians 1–2, as part of the provision to access greater works. Thus the revival journey continues. Along the way I have failed, but the Holy Spirit patiently keeps cultivating and nurturing faith. Praise God, *there is more!*

Summary of the Phases of Revival:

1 Phase One: There Must Be More!

2 Phase Two: Seeking God's Reviving Presence

3 Phase Three: God Has Come!

4 Phase Four: Brokenness: The Way Into Blessing

5 Phase Five: Life Again!

*The*REVIVAL
JOURNEY

THE REVIVAL ROAD

*T*he revival road is both a road to revival and a road of revival. This final chapter addresses various aspects of both emphases. Also included in this discussion are several important related issues.

THE ROAD TO REVIVAL

The road to revival consists of five phases. This book has detailed each phase in the previous five chapters. However, a simple review noting further observations may aid in a deeper grasp of these revival truths.

Review of Reverse Order

The order taken in this book has actually been in reverse order in an effort to bring people to the starting point of There Must Be More!

The reverse order is as follows: Phase Five is *Life Again!* But what is the way into this blessing of revival? Phase Four is *Brokenness: The Way into Blessing*. But what brings people to genuine brokenness? Phase Three is *God Has Come!* But when does God come manifesting His reviving presence? Phase Two is *Seeking God's Reviving Presence*. But why and when do people seek God—and especially His reviving presence? Phase One is *There Must Be More!*

Review of Natural Order

Phase One is when a believer or believers realize that *There Must Be More!* This awakening is an awareness or conviction of need as well as of the Father's ability to meet that need. Phase Two naturally follows as those awakened begin *Seeking God's Reviving Presence*. Essentially, this seeking is expressed in the cry for deliverance. God promises to hear this humble cry. Phase Three is therefore that *God Has Come!* This is the outpouring of the Spirit: the spiritual, powerful manifestation of the presence of God. Phase Four is the right response to this convicting presence of God as people are brought to *Brokenness: The Way into Blessing*. This is honesty before a holy God, who blesses the humility of honesty. Phase Five is therefore the promised blessing of *Life Again!* God heals the brokenhearted by restoring them back to spiritual life—life in the Spirit. These five phases delineate the road *to* revival.

Illustration of the Revival Journey: The Prodigal Son

As mentioned in Chapter One, the parable of the prodigal son, found in Luke 15:11–32, incorporates the New Testament word for revival, *anazao*. While it is legitimate to apply this parable to the lost getting saved, it is significant to note that the son is called a *son* and the father is of course called the *father*. Therefore the interpretation of the parable is dealing with a prodigal son in the sense of a child of God who is estranged from his Heavenly Father being revived (Luke 15:24a, 32a).[1] However, this is like someone who is "lost" being "found" (Luke 15:24b, 32b).

Luke 15:11–16 describes the backslidden condition of the prodigal, who wasted his inheritance in a selfish and wicked lifestyle. Then when he ran out of resources, a famine also arose in the land. In need, but still attempting to solve his own problems, he took a job feeding pigs (truly a low job for a Jew). Luke 15:16 describes his hunger and need by saying, "And he would fain have filled his belly with the husks that the swine did eat: and no man gave unto him." He was so in need that he was literally tempted to eat the pigs' food.

Jesus then says in the next verse, "And when he came to himself, he said, How many hired servants of my father's have bread enough and to spare, and I perish with hunger!"—*There Must Be More!* Finally the prodigal awakened to his need and the resources of his father. This is always the first phase.

Immediately, the prodigal responded by saying, "I will arise and go to my father, and will say unto him, Father, I have sinned against heaven, and before thee, And am no more worthy to be called thy son: make me as one of thy hired servants. And he arose, and came to his father" (Luke 15:18–20a).

The prodigal sought his father. This expresses the second phase: *Seeking God's Reviving Presence.*

The prodigal's planned "speech" revealed an admission of his need. In a sense this is the first stage of brokenness as he admitted, "I need help!" This was a confession, but as of yet primarily a confession of his need.

The story continues, "But when he was yet a great way off, his father saw him, and had compassion, and ran, and fell on his neck, and kissed him" (Luke 15:20*b*). This meeting with the father beautifully pictures the third phase: *God Has Come!* In fact, the word translated *fell* is the same word used in the book of Acts of the Holy Spirit "falling" on people, describing the outpouring of the Spirit (Acts 8:16; 10:44; 11:15).

This aspect of the story of the prodigal son illustrates the revival truth "Draw nigh to God, and he will draw nigh to you" (James 4:8). As the son "came to his father," his father "ran" to meet him. What a beautiful picture of the loving Heavenly Father! God prefers to deliver—to revive—rather than to judge.

This response of the father brought his son to the fourth phase: *Brokenness: The Way into Blessing.* Remember the son's planned speech: "Father, I have sinned against heaven, and before thee, And am no more worthy to be called thy son: *make me as one of thy hired servants*"—so that his needs could be met. But this is not what he said to his father. Luke 15:21 reveals, "And the son said unto him, Father, I have sinned against

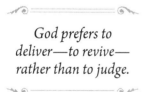

God prefers to deliver—to revive—rather than to judge.

heaven, and in thy sight, and am no more worthy to be called thy son"—and he stopped, never finishing the last planned phrase. He was truly broken. He did not focus on his need (first stage of brokenness—confession of need); he focused on his sin (second stage of brokenness—confession of sin).

This was true brokenness: "I have sinned ... and am no more worthy to be called thy son." Many accounts of revival depict these "two stages of brokenness": the first one leading up to the greater outpouring of the Spirit as a part of the seeking phase and the second one following the manifested presence of God.

This fourth phase of brokenness led to revival blessing. Luke 15:22–23 explains that the father called for new clothing for the repentant son ("the best robe"), new identification ("a ring"), and new footwear ("and shoes on his feet")—all picturing a fresh "cleansing" and restoration.

Then the father called for a feast ("the fatted calf") and rejoicing ("be merry"), picturing a fresh "filling." In fact, in Luke 15:24 the father said, "For this my son was dead, and is *alive again*." The son was not dead physically. Therefore the issue was spiritual. "Alive again" translates from the word *anazao*. The prodigal son was no longer prodigal. He was experiencing the final revival phase: *Life Again!*

"And they began to be merry" (Luke 15:24*b*). God rejoices when His children are revived. The pilgrimage of the prodigal beautifully illustrates the revival journey.

The Divine and Human Elements

It is the Holy Spirit who convicts man of his need that *there must be more!* It is man who must then exercise faith by *seeking God's reviving presence.* God then responds by pouring out His Spirit, described as *God has come!* Man's responsibility then is *brokenness: the way into blessing.* But it is God who then infuses *life again!* Throughout this divine/human dynamic, God responds to those who respond to Him! God is always the one who initiates and enables anything good. But man must respond in faith to God's initiations in order to be blessed by His enablements. It must be remembered that faith is not a work. Faith simply responds to and depends on the Worker.

The Definition of Revival

Revival, in its simplest sense, is a restoration to spiritual life—the life of God or life in the Spirit.

Chapter One expanded this simple definition to articulate the various levels of revival. *Personal Revival is a restoration to spiritual life in the sense of a saint being restored to the Spirit-filled life.* This sense of revival speaks strictly of the individual level. *Corporate Revival is a restoration to spiritual life in the sense of the saints being restored to the Spirit-led and Spirit-enabled function of a body of believers.* This sense of revival moves beyond one individual to a group of believers functioning in the Spirit together as one body. *A Revival of Religion is a restoration to spiritual life in the sense of the unsaved being restored to the original plan of God indwelling man.* This sense of revival moves beyond impacting the saints to impacting the lost. *General Revival is a restoration to spiritual life in the sense of a people in a broad area being restored to the life of God.* This sense of revival includes the impact among the saved and unsaved in a large geographical area.

All of these definitions focus on the narrow sense of revival, which is man's received blessing—*life again.* However, revival may be defined with a focus on the broad sense of revival, which is God's divine moving—*the outpouring of the Spirit.*

Chapter Three explained this broader concept of revival. The outpouring of the Spirit is the spiritual, powerful manifestation of the presence of God. The phrase *the outpouring of the Spirit* focuses on God's divine moving, while the word *revival*, in its narrow sense, focuses on man's received blessing. However, broadly the word *revival* may be used to include both concepts.

The issue is *life* (*vive*)—God's life or God's presence. God's presence (life) *to* believers (the outpouring of the Spirit) leads to God's presence (life) *through* believers (the filling of the Spirit). The outpouring of the Spirit is God's presence manifested in the atmosphere. The filling of the Spirit is God's presence manifested in the believer.

In a narrow sense, revival is the reality of Phase Five: *Life Again!* In a broad sense, revival is the reality of Phase Three: *God Has Come!* In a yet broader sense, revival is the combination of Phases Three, Four, and Five: *God Has Come! Brokenness: The Way into Blessing*, and then *Life Again!* Therefore, in the broadest sense, *revival is the spiritual, powerful manifestation of the presence of God that leads the saints to brokenness and a restoration to spiritual life and that awakens the lost to a reception of eternal life.*

> *Therefore, in the broadest sense,* revival is the spiritual, powerful manifestation of the presence of God that leads the saints to brokenness and a restoration to spiritual life and that awakens the lost to a reception of eternal life.

In the matter of defining revival, there are two prevalent misconceptions. First, some confuse what revival *is* with what revival *does*. The subsequent danger is a "struggle theology" in pursuing revival. This was discussed in detail in Chapter One.

Second, some confuse the outpouring of the Spirit with the filling of the Spirit as if both were the same. However, as just noted above, the former is more of a cause, and the latter is more of an effect when there is a right response to the cause.

THE WIDENING CIRCLES OF REVIVAL

In Chapters One and Three, issues of extent were discussed. Little fires beget larger fires. Faith for personal revival precedes faith for greater revival. Often personal revival spreads to a few others, resulting in a small group revival. Sometimes these revived ones whose faith has been strengthened become the intercessors for a church-wide revival. Churches may then become the intercessors for a community-wide revival and so forth. As the circle widens, there is both a gratitude for what has occurred as well as a cry for more—blessing for others.

The issue of extent involves both the outpouring of the Spirit (God's divine moving) and revival (man's received blessing). For example, the Lewis Revival (1949–1953) actually came as a result of the widening circles of revival beginning at least eighteen months before December 1949, when the greater blessing came.

In 1948 Peggy and Christine Smith, two elderly sisters, began to sense a need for another visitation from on high on the Isle of Lewis, which is off the northwest coast of Scotland. Although Lewis was a "land of revivals," the last revival had occurred in 1939, nine years before. Therefore a new generation of young people did not know experientially the power of God displayed in the 1939 revival. As these ladies prayed several times a week in their humble cottage, one particular night they became convinced of the promise of Isaiah 44:3, "I will pour water upon him that is thirsty." The convincement came through the outpouring of the Spirit on their little prayer meeting of two. They testified later to Duncan Campbell: "We had a consciousness of God that created a confidence in our souls which refused to accept defeat."[2]

Confident of God's promise, the ladies contacted their pastor, James MacKay, claiming that revival was coming and urging him to meet together with the leading men in order to intercede for the coming blessing.[3] For several months the men prayed. Then on one occasion as they prayed in a barn, a young deacon rose and read from Psalm 24:

> "Who shall ascend into the hill of the Lord? Or who shall stand in his holy place? He that hath clean hands and a pure heart; who hath not lifted up his soul unto vanity, nor sworn deceitfully. He shall receive the blessing from the Lord."

> Turning to the others, he said, "Brethren, it seems to me just so much humbug to be waiting and praying as we are if we ourselves are not rightly related to God." Then lifting his hands toward heaven, he cried: "Oh God, are *my* hands clean? Is *my* heart pure?"

> He got no further but fell prostrate to the floor. An awareness of God filled the barn, and a stream of supernatural power was let loose in their lives. They had moved into a new sphere of God-realization, believing implicitly in the promise of revival."[4]

The circle had widened in power from two to a small group as God poured out His Spirit on the praying men. With hearts revived and faith greatly strengthened, these men continued in intercession with the same expectation as the two sisters, trusting God to do what He had promised to do. Finally sensing that God was ready to move in a greater way, they invited Duncan Campbell to come in December of 1949 to the village church in Barvas. After several nights, "God stepped down from heaven," and both the church and community were confronted with the presence of God.

Again the circle had widened to the church-wide and community-wide levels of extent. Eventually village after village throughout the Isle of Lewis knew the reviving presence of God. Campbell preached throughout Lewis largely for the next three years. Therefore again the circle had widened to the region of the Isle of Lewis. The Lewis Revival is a beautiful example of the widening circles of revival.

When speaking of corporate revival, it should be noted that those involved in the early circles of revival participate in all five phases of the revival journey; however, those involved in the later (wider) circles of revival participate primarily in the last three phases of the revival journey.

THE PATHWAY OF CONTINUOUS REVIVAL

Continuous revival involves both the corporate and individual levels.

Corporate Continuous Revival

What accesses revival is what continues revival. The Second Great Awakening is a remarkable example of this. America, after the American Revolution, manifested great spiritual need by the 1780s. Immigration brought multitudes that knew not the power of the First Great Awakening. Anti-God and anti-Bible literature was being disseminated. Drunkenness and immorality had spiraled to incredibly high percentages. Yet in the midst of this declension God was quietly working. A few small fires burned. In 1795 those burdened sent out a call to prayer by circulating the "Circular Letter." This letter challenged churches to institute a "Concert of Prayer" by designating one day per quarter (eventually this became one day per month) as a day to seek God's reviving presence. By 1798 the little fires were fanned by the Wind of the Spirit into big fires, and the revival became general. Over the years it spread down the eastern seaboard and into the western states of that era, affecting churches and colleges. The key to the continuous revival was the continuous concert of prayer. In fact, when the fires began to die down in the late 1820s, word was sent out in 1830 to increase the intensity of the "Concert of Prayer."

What accesses revival is what continues revival.

Almost immediately the fires burned brightly again. The two greatest seasons of the revival were the early 1820s and early 1830s. The revival lasted into the early 1840s.

It is no accident that as the "Concert of Prayer" continued along with the regular preaching that the Second Great Awakening lasted over four decades. J. Edwin Orr chronicles the continuous prayer movement with the continuous revival in his book *The Eager Feet: Evangelical Awakenings, 1790–1830*.[5]

Personal Continuous Revival

The pathway of continuous revival on the individual level involves a "walk." The nature of walking implies a continuation. Walking is simply reiterated steps. Therefore the walk of revival is just one step at a time. A backward focus on the past—wallowing in past failure—or a forward focus on the future—fearing a misstep—will hinder in the present step. If one presently takes the right step, God will presently enable. What are the right steps? The steps to enter into revival are the steps to continue in revival.

Walking in the Light

Walking in the light as God is in the light is walking in the light of Holy Spirit conviction (I John 1:7). It is brokenness in the light of seeing oneself in some measure from God's perspective. This was discussed in detail in Chapter Two. The simple steps on this pathway of walking in the light are confession and faith (I John 1:9). Confession is honesty before the God who knows all, and faith is taking the promised forgiveness, cleansing, and restoration. The result is a clean heart opening the way for a filled life.

Walking in the Spirit

As someone receives Christ by surrendering to the conviction of the Holy Spirit and thus trusting in Christ as one's Savior, one is to "walk . . . in him" (Col. 2:6). Therefore walking in Christ or "walking in the Spirit" is simply surrendering to the Spirit's leadership and depending on His enablement to obey for each step. The simple steps on the pathway of walking in the Spirit are surrender and faith. When the steps of surrender and faith are taken, "ye shall not fulfil the lust of the flesh" (Gal. 5:16). This is the reality of "I live; yet not I, but Christ" by "faith" (Gal. 2:20). It is the Spirit filling one with the life of Christ, which is the Spirit-filled life. This is spiritual life—continuous revival.

When one depends on the Spirit's leadership and enablement, he is depending or believing on Christ. Jesus said, "He that believeth on me, as the scripture hath said, out of his belly [from his innermost being] shall flow rivers of living water. (But this spake he of the Spirit)" (John 7:38–39a). This is as simple as "he that believeth on me hath everlasting life" (John 6:47). In fact, the condition is exactly the same: *he that believeth*. However, the purpose varies: one, to receive eternal life (the Fountain), the other to access the abundant life (the filling). *He that believeth* is the simple condition for both salvation and the Spirit-filled life, regardless of one's feeling or "experience." As one simply trusts Christ to do what He promised, Christ does it—whether it is the granting of eternal life or the impartation of the abundant life.

Walking in the light is how to deal with sin. Walking in the Spirit is how to keep from sin. If one stumbles by yielding to his flesh, he simply needs to immediately walk in the light again. God will immediately cleanse and restore. Then he must immediately walk in the Spirit, and the Spirit will immediately enable. This double emphasis of truth is the revival road on the individual level. It is stepping onto the road of faith in order to grow in grace without hindrance.

Roy Hession's *The Calvary Road* and *We Would See Jesus* expand these two emphases with clarity and illustration from real revival.[6]

THE DISCIPLESHIP OF REVIVAL

Revival must be discipled. This overlaps somewhat with the previous point of continuous revival. The point here is that care must be taken to stoke the fires of revival. As those who receive eternal life (salvation) need discipleship, so those who are restored to spiritual life (revival) need discipleship. Discipleship demands fueling the fires of faith and guarding the fires of faith.

Instruction in revival truth fuels the fires of faith by focusing on the foundation for faith. Faith always comes by hearing and hearing by the Word of God (Rom. 10:17). Therefore there is the need for the continued imbibing of truth. Even once a truth is powerfully learned, one must keep renewing his mind in that very truth (Rom. 12:2). Otherwise, truth fades because of human frailty. Therefore discipleship involves a focus on the various grace-facts and grace-promises that may be accessed through faith-choices. This is a focus on the victorious provision available in Christ.

> *Revival must be discipled… Discipleship demands fueling the fires of faith and guarding the fires of faith.*

Sensitivity to the Holy Spirit in separation (holiness) guards the fires of faith by providing the protection of faith.

Separation from the world regards that which could hinder revival from continuing. Yielding to the flesh immediately stops the previous yielding to the Spirit. Whatever one sows to the flesh will of the flesh reap corruption (Gal. 6:8). Therefore, yielding to the Spirit regarding separation from the world becomes more important than some may realize.

Separation from the world presents new surrenders, and surrender and faith keep one on the revival road. The revived life sensitizes one's conscience. If one then goes against his conscience, he hurts his faith because he is going against what he *believes* is right. Therefore violating one's conscience shipwrecks one's faith (I Tim. 1:19). If this occurs, the revival dies because the revived life of walking in the Spirit is on the basis of walking by faith. So surrender to the Spirit regarding matters of separation protects faith.

Separation needs revival for life. However, revival needs separation for biblical boundaries. Either one without the other disintegrates. However, it must be kept in mind that the motivation for separation must always be love for Christ—the unbroken fellowship of the Holy Spirit. It is possible for the flesh to attempt self-dependent separation and therefore be proud in its motivation for separation. This leads to condescension of others. Anything of the flesh would obviously hinder revival.

Instruction in revival truth is needed to disciple revival because it focuses on the foundation for faith; sensitivity to the Holy Spirit in separation is needed to disciple revival because it provides the protection of faith. Faith is the key in both walking in the light and walking in the Spirit.

Therefore discipleship involves fueling the fires of faith as well as guarding the fires of faith.

The Dangers of Revival

Revival focuses on seeking God and accessing the life of God. Therefore Satan hates revival because Satan hates God. As long as God's people are fleshly, either through unrighteousness or self-righteousness, Satan does not mind.

But when God's people become clothed with God, Satan knows his kingdom of darkness is about to get plundered. When God's people experience revival, Satan's "turf" is threatened, and therefore he attacks revival on all levels and through various means. This section will address several of Satan's attacks.[7]

False Conclusions

One of Satan's attacks involves wrong conclusions regarding revival either before revival comes or after it has come.

Before Revival

Some conclude that if revival comes, everything and everyone will be "sorted out." While it is true that God's reviving presence is surely the answer, it must be remembered that victory is never automatic. Victory is by faith. Those involved are responsible to respond rightly to God's working. It is possible for some to resist the Holy Spirit. In fact, the Enemy will do all he can to hinder and oppose revival. As a result, revival at times may include some nearly disillusioning aspects if one is without understanding.

R. A. Torrey clarified this in the following:

Many a church is praying for a revival that does not really desire a revival. They think they do, for to their minds a revival means an increase of membership, an increase of income, an increase of reputation among the churches, but if they knew what a real revival meant, what a searching of hearts on the part of professed Christians would be involved, what a radical transformation of individual, domestic, and social life would be brought about, and many other things that would come to pass if the Spirit of God was poured out in reality and power; if all this were known, the real cry of the church would be:

"O God, keep us from having a revival."

Many a minister is praying for the baptism with the Holy Spirit [personal revival] who does not really desire it. He thinks he does, for the baptism with the Spirit means to him new joy, new power in preaching the Word, a wider reputation among men, a larger prominence in the church of Christ. But if he understood what a baptism with the Holy Spirit really involved, how for example it would necessarily bring him into antagonism with the world, and with unspiritual Christians, how it would cause his name to be "cast out as evil," how it might necessitate his leaving a good comfortable living and going down to work in the slums, or even in some foreign land; if he understood all this, his prayer quite likely would be—if he were to express the real wish of his heart,—

"O God, save me from being baptized with the Holy Ghost."

But when we do come to the place where we really desire the conversion of friends at any cost, really desire the outpouring of the Holy Spirit whatever it may involve, really desire the baptism with the Holy Ghost come what may, where we desire anything "in truth" and then call upon God for it "in truth," God is going to hear.[8]

After Revival

First, some conclude that because they were favored with revival, they are "better" than others who have not been so favored. Pride is a danger to any blessed people. Although man is responsible to exercise faith, faith is not a work, and to conclude that one has in any way merited God's favor in revival is arrogant. Revival is always a matter of God's mercy (Hab. 3:2). Pride also opens people to other satanic attacks, which may include attacks in the moral realm. Great caution must therefore be exercised to walk humbly before God.

Second, some conclude that because they were favored with revival, it justifies all their doctrines or practices. However, the blessing of revival simply means that God blessed someone's faith. It does not follow that God is placing His stamp of approval on all that one believes or does. Every doctrine and every practice must be weighed according to the scales of scriptural truth.

Third, some who are surprised by revival conclude that revival is an arbitrary choice of God to favor His people. However, this false conclusion, which is really fatalism, reveals that those who come to this conclusion are not involved in the faith-filled intercession for revival. The intercessors in a revival are not "surprised." Rather, the intercessors are expecting God to be true to His Word according to Holy Spirit convincement.

Opposition

Another attack from Satan is simply to oppose those on the revival road. Just as a new convert is shocked when his family and friends may not readily accept the Savior as he just did and may even oppose him, so likewise one who enters the revival road may be shocked that others do not readily join the journey and may even oppose him. Within local churches there may be a polarization that takes place. Many prefer "controlled carnality" to real fervent Christianity. When revival takes place, if some resist the work of God while others surrender, over time the difference between the two groups will become a stark contrast.

Those who oppose revival do so usually for one of two reasons: worldliness or self-righteousness. Worldliness is conformity to the world's selfish desires in heart and life, evidenced by the works of the flesh. Self-righteousness is conformity to any standard of righteousness maintained through the strength of the flesh. Just as justification by faith confronts both unrighteous sinners and self-righteous sinners, so sanctification by faith or revival confronts both worldly saints and self-righteous saints. And just as justification by faith is resisted by both the unrighteous—who do not want their sin to be exposed as a problem—and the self-righteous—who do not want their "filthy rags" to be exposed as insufficient—so sanctification by faith or revival is resisted by both the worldly saints—who do not want their worldliness to be challenged—and the self-righteous saints—who do not want their condition of self-righteous rags to be challenged either.

> *In times of revival, the worldly react to holiness, and the self-righteous react to the Holy Spirit.*

In times of revival, the worldly react to holiness, and the self-righteous react to the Holy Spirit. Those in the former group accuse those on the revival road of placing too much emphasis on holiness. Those in the latter group accuse those on the revival road of placing too much emphasis on the Holy Spirit.

In local church settings, those who resist revival may attack the pastor. This is usually done by either magnifying petty issues to monumental proportions (Satan loves the tactic of distortion) or by accusing the pastor of being somehow "doctrinally off." The results for the cause of Christ in some cases may be tragic.

The revival road may involve becoming "the off-scouring of all things" (I Cor. 4:13) in the eyes of others. But God uses even this to help those seeking His face to die to reputation. Death to self always accesses more of the life of Christ.

Counterfeit Revival

Counterfeit revival, another of Satan's tactics, generally manifests itself in two possible forms and at times includes both.

Imitation

Some sincere souls read accounts of revivals and attempt to imitate the incidents in a given scenario without stopping to discern what is essential and what is incidental. The genuine work of God is a real blessing, even when it takes a person out of his comfort zone. But imitations of the real thing are "sickening" to those with spiritual perception.

Also sometimes people desire to implement good things, such as revival prayer meetings, and try to imitate the exact details of a particular story, such as having the prayer meetings at a certain time. However, the key is obeying the Holy Spirit in all details.

Strange Fire

The other form of counterfeit revival includes demonic involvement. This can occur individually or in the corporate setting. Individually, when someone surrenders all to God, he opens himself up to the supernatural realm. However, if he does not understand that in the supernatural realm there is the Holy Spirit and there are evil spirits, he may embrace anything in that realm as if it were the Holy Spirit. In this way, the Enemy may eventually lead well-meaning souls into that which discredits the cause of Christ. This caution must be understood and heeded by seekers of revival.

Corporately, if Satan cannot keep people from revival, he may attempt to push them to excesses in revival in an effort to discredit the revival. Therefore leaders in a revival need biblical and spiritual discernment. For example, in the Congo Revival of the 1950s, the leaders decided that if a "phenomenon" occurred that could be found in Scripture they would allow it, but if not they would restrain it. Another example regards the First Great Awakening. Where degrading phenomena occurred, as in people barking like dogs, leaders like George Whitefield rejected it and did not promote it, but leaders like James Davenport accepted it and promoted it. Consequently, revival fires burned brightly in Whitefield's ministry but were quenched in Davenport's, proving that degrading phenomena is a satanic counterfeit.

This degrading type of phenomena is much different than the effects on a human frame when one is given a view of his sin and eternal realities. This may cause "phenomena," but it will not be degrading.

However, phenomena are not essential to revival. Rather they are incidental in that they may or may not occur. The true test of a work of God is not whether or not there are phenomena, but whether the work passes the tests of I John 4. To "try [test] the spirits" (4:1), several questions may be asked: Does the work promote a right view toward Christ? The Spirit of Christ is for Christ and against Satan and the world (4:2–5). Does the work promote a right view toward the Scriptures? The Spirit of truth urges obedience to the truth, not disobedience (4:6). Does the work promote a right view toward others? The Spirit of love sheds abroad the love of God in and through the hearts of believers, encouraging attitudes of Christlikeness and actions of service (4:7–18).[9]

Wise leaders of revival never promote phenomena. Rather they scripturally and spiritually discern what to accept and what to reject.

Unbelief

A further attack on revival is Satan's attempt to pull God's people off the position of faith into unbelief. Some who pursue revival in an extent greater than personal revival may become disillusioned if revival does not come on their timetable. Personal revival may be accessed immediately, but corporate revival involves other factors. God is ready to bless a ready people. However, some are deceived as to their readiness. God knows when seeking hearts are truly ready.

But as God seeks to purify and test or prove faith, Satan seeks to discourage people into unbelief.

Sometimes there may be an area of un-surrender that hinders someone pursuing revival. God patiently seeks to reveal this. But if someone continues in un-surrender, it always hinders faith for greater revival.

Some may seek the Lord with half-heartedness. Delay tests the hearts. If one is fine if God pours out His Spirit and fine if He does not, then he is willing to be satisfied with life as it is. This reveals a lack of wholeheartedness and shows a mixed heart. A whole heart is set on God's reviving presence as the answer for those for whom he is burdened. Obviously, the practical aspects of life must be tended to, but a whole or "perfect" heart is fixed on one aim—for God to show Himself strong through the outpouring of His Spirit.

Some may seek the Lord with short-termed faith. Delay proves convincement of God's promise and produces enduring faith. God is glorified as the intercessors affirm the ground God has given in the spiritual realm and trust God to rend the heavens and bring the answer into the physical realm. Long-termed or enduring faith ultimately obtains God's promise (Heb. 10:36).

The study of revival history reveals that if there has not been a revival in a greater extent for a long period of time, the seeking phase may take longer. Those seeking are probing new territory. This slows the process of faith since God must teach the seekers necessary lessons to prepare their hearts. But as lessons of faith are learned, faith is strengthened for greater works, hearts are purged from wrong motives, convincement is proved, and channels are made ready for God to work through and learn not to take the glory. When God pours out His Spirit, many others join in and see near immediate blessing, having no concept of the time and "death" that it took for the original intercessors. A classic example of this is the revival journey of Marie Monsen. Her story involved a twenty-year pilgrimage that ultimately saw great revival in China. One small spring of life grew to a flood-tide of blessing.[10]

THE PROMOTION OF REVIVAL

Although there may at times be abuses in "promoting" revival, there are biblical responsibilities and therefore legitimate "means" to promote revival.

Revival Preaching

In a certain sense, the overarching biblical method in promoting revival is faith-filled preaching. God's plan is to use "the foolishness of preaching" as the tool to accomplish His work. This preaching of the Word must be faith-filled so that it is Spirit-filled and divinely enabled to penetrate hearts. God uses the preaching of truth to ignite and fuel revival.

> *Although there may at times be abuses in "promoting" revival, there are biblical responsibilities and therefore legitimate "means" to promote revival.*

Specific, confrontational, urgent preaching that is based on the authority of the Word, intended to persuade, and filled with instruction—this is revival preaching. It is focused preaching, focusing on man's problem of sin separating between him and God and focusing on God's provision in Christ as the all-sufficient answer to man's need.

Preaching for revival is awakening preaching so that the audience awakens to the great fact that *There Must Be More!* Preaching for revival is a call to prayer so that the hearers begin *Seeking God's Reviving Presence.* Preaching for revival is self-denying, Christ-uplifting, devil-banishing preaching through which God often delights to rend the heavens and come down so that all cry out *God Has Come!* Preaching for revival is incisive preaching demanding a verdict so that accompanied by the manifest presence of God, it brings people to *Brokenness: The Way into Blessing.* Preaching for revival is instructive preaching, explaining the reality and the continued access of *Life Again!* Revival preaching is a necessary essential to revival.

Revival Praying

In another sense, faith-filled praying is the overarching biblical method in promoting revival. For without the prayer of faith that accesses the Spirit's ministry in, on, and through the preaching, the preaching has no power. Praying for revival is not prayer-dependence (works), it is God-dependence (faith), and faith accesses grace (Rom. 5:2). Revival praying is that which accesses God's blessing on the revival preaching that God uses in the phases of revival just noted. Therefore, broadly, revival praying affects all the phases of revival by impacting revival preaching. Narrowly, revival praying is predominant in the second phase of *Seeking God's Reviving Presence* (praying for revival) and largely in the fourth phase of *Brokenness: The Way into Blessing* (praying in revival). Many times God has delighted to rend the heavens and come down in a corporate time of seeking His face. Revival praying is also a necessary essential to revival.

Revival Praying and Revival Preaching

Revival preaching without revival praying lacks power. However, revival praying without revival preaching lacks "detonation." But revival praying with revival preaching is explosive. Acts 1–2 is a classic example of this glorious dynamic.

Therefore it is really the combination of revival praying with revival preaching that is the overarching biblical method in promoting revival. These two emphases refer to man's responsibility or the means of promoting revival. Yet *the* essential to revival is the revival Presence—God Himself.

May the saints in each generation know experientially revival praying, revival preaching, and most importantly— the revival Presence!

CONCLUSION

"God works from the midst of a Spirit-filled people out upon the world. All who long for worldwide revival must see to it that they hasten the day by personally entering the Spirit-filled life, while congregations must seek—what may never have entered their minds before as possible—to have their Pentecost."[11]

For those with a heart for revival, who are desirous of having their motives purified, and who are willing to die to self— revival is God's promised blessing. Who will utterly abandon himself to God by embarking on the revival journey?

Appendix A

A SYMPHONY
OF PRAYER

As a young elementary student, I went on a school field trip to Orchestra Hall to hear the Chicago Symphony play. Although we sat in one of the higher balconies, the harmonious sound was magnificent. In the musical realm there is something special about a symphony orchestra.

In Matthew 18:19–20, the Lord Jesus uses the concept of a symphony to instruct believers regarding corporate prayer: "Again I say unto you, That if two of you shall agree on earth as touching any thing that they shall ask, it shall be done for them of my Father which is in heaven. For where two or three are gathered together in my name, there am I in the midst of them." In these two verses Christ explains the basic concept of a symphony of prayer. He begins with a condition, follows with a promise, and finishes with a reason.

THE CONDITION OF SYMPHONIZED PRAYER

The word *If* in verse 19 introduces the conditional clause: "If two of you shall agree on earth as touching any thing that they shall ask." Two key words, *agree* and *ask*, explain the condition.

Agreement

First, *agree* is translated from the word *sumphoneo*, literally meaning "to produce a sound together."[1] A symphony orchestra is made up of many instruments, but as each musician follows the conductor, based upon the musical score, together they produce a pleasing symphony of sound. Likewise, a corporate prayer meeting incorporates many instruments of God's people, but as each one follows the conductor of the Holy Spirit, based upon the score of God's Word, together they produce a harmonious symphony of prayer. Therefore it is important for each instrument to look to the Holy Spirit for leadership. As the Holy Spirit brings issues to mind and burdens one's spirit, one may know it is his cue to symphonize in prayer.

Spiritual Reality

The spiritual reality of a symphony of prayer generally follows three "movements."

A Symphony of Burden

A symphony of prayer begins with a symphony of burden based on man's need. As this one cries out his burden, the Holy Spirit concurs in another's heart that "this heart cry is of God." Immediately that one cries out the same burden, perhaps adding more details. Others sense in their spirit the leading of the Holy Spirit and symphonize with the burden by crying out as well.

A Symphony of Faith

A symphony of burden leads (sometimes quickly, sometimes through protracted periods of time) to a symphony of faith based on God's promise. The Spirit begins to bear witness with someone's spirit, convincing him of God's will based on God's truth. As that one rises in faith, expressing the "evidence" of the foundation for faith, others sense the same convincement from the Lord. Faith spreads. They then symphonize in faith one by one. The whole meeting then rises to a new level. This is one of the great blessings of a corporate prayer meeting: it allows faith to be cultivated in many hearts—sometimes in ways that would have been missed in one's individual prayer life. When many are convinced of the Spirit's leading, one is protected from second-guessing his own individual convincement.

A Symphony of Praise

Eventually, as transactions of faith are made, the symphony of faith can rise to a symphony of praise based on biblical expectation. The Holy Spirit has granted divine convincement. Prayers of faith have been transacted. At that point for those particular issues, promises have been received. Therefore the ground of faith must simply be asserted, praising God for what He has done and looking forward to the fulfillment of the matter.

Practical Ramifications

A true symphony of prayer demands several practical considerations for the individuals involved.

Be Focused

How can a group agree or symphonize in prayer if each participant is not focused? The nature of a symphony demands that each instrument be focused and ready to play its part. It is impossible to symphonize if each individual is not focused on the symphony.

When I was an assistant to my father, every Saturday morning we had a men's prayer breakfast. Thankfully, we did have some men who knew how to pray. New converts also were invited to this special prayer time. Once a new convert asked me, "When the men are praying, why do others make sounds?" I said, "You mean like 'Amen!' or 'Yes, Lord'?" He responded, "Well, that too, but I mean not even words, just sounds." I said, "You mean like . . ." and demonstrated a deep groan. He said excitedly, "Yes, that's it—what are they doing?" I explained that while one man is praying, the others are listening and praying with the one who is verbally leading. Sometimes they may say, "Amen!" or "Yes, Lord." But sometimes they may just groan their agreement to what is being prayed. He said with enlightenment, "Oh, okay." In the next men's prayer time, as one man was praying I heard this new convert groan a hearty agreement. He was learning the importance of focus in corporate prayer.

Be Brief

One reason for brevity in corporate prayer meetings is that long prayers often cause others to lose focus and start daydreaming. This hinders the symphony. Also, if someone just "prays down through his list," there is no opportunity to symphonize as the Spirit burdens. It may be that the first request was of the Lord. Others may sense the burden to symphonize. But if the first person just keeps going routinely down his list, the burden others received will be lost by the time he finishes his list.

In a symphony of prayer, each individual must pray only the burden that the Holy Spirit leads. Obviously throughout the symphony, the Holy Spirit may lead individuals to pray more than once. In contrast, when each one in a prayer meeting prays "his prayer," the prayer is usually longer because people feel like they must have something to say. This element risks a flesh-driven prayer. However, shorter prayers in obedience to the Spirit cultivate sensitivity to the Spirit's actual leading.

Understandably, "brief" varies for different people. Also, when just a few folk are on are their faces before God about a specific matter, brief may be a "longer brief." But when a larger group is praying together, brief should generally be a "shorter brief." If one person drones on, although he may be intellectually stimulated, the droning prayer is deadening to others. Sometimes the Spirit may initially give life to the one praying, but when the Spirit stops, the one praying keeps going. Then an effort is made to create the life sensed in the first part of the prayer. This, of course, is the flesh. The key is to follow the Holy Spirit.

D. L. Moody once asked a preacher to lead in prayer at the beginning of a gospel service. An agnostic who had wandered in out of curiosity was about to leave because the prayer meandered on and on. Moody wisely stepped up to the pulpit and said something to the effect of the following: "While our brother finishes his prayer, let's all take our hymnals and turn to a song!" The agnostic was so impressed with how Moody handled this situation that he stayed and through it came to Christ.

Let Requests Be Voiced in Prayer

Much time is often lost as prayer requests are taken. Although there may be appropriate times for this method, a symphony of prayer is looking to the Holy Spirit to lead and burden as the prayer meeting moves along. The desire is to let the Spirit orchestrate a symphony of burden based on need and so forth. As the Holy Spirit leads, requests will be voiced in prayer, and then others may symphonize. In the end, the requests are made known, but without the loss of a "prayer request" time.

Guard Against Distractions

Distractions cause people to break focus. When focus is broken, the purpose of symphonized prayer is lost. Some things may be unavoidable. However with pre-thought, many distractions could and should be avoided. This is helpful since the Holy Spirit works through our faculties, not around them.

Speak Loudly Enough for the Size of the Group

Again the reason is so that all can enter into the reality of corporate prayer. When the one praying cannot be heard, others cannot symphonize with him in prayer. A reminder of this at the beginning of a prayer time is helpful.

Participate as the Holy Spirit Leads

Generally in a corporate setting, the Spirit will lead many to participate. Just as a symphony orchestra uses many instruments, a symphony of prayer uses many voices. Since prayer is not a matter of instructing, women, young people, and even children may participate. The prayer meeting in Acts 1 was specifically "with the women" (Acts 1:14). Also I Corinthians 11 definitely implies women praying in the assembly. In fact, the tenderness of women often helps pride to be set aside for all involved.

It may be asked, "What if you are not in tune?" The answer is simple: "Get tuned up before you start." Before orchestras begin, they take the time to all get in tune. The same is true spiritually. Personally, I have had times when I sensed a spiritual dullness as we began a prayer meeting. Yet when asking the Lord to search me and tune me up, He faithfully brings to light that which needs to be adjusted.

God can even tune people up physically. One New Year's Eve I was in Ireland. I had just flown through the night, getting only about three hours of sleep on the flight. I stayed busy all day to get myself accustomed to the new time zone. Then, since it was New Year's Eve, we went to a prayer meeting which was to last as long as the Lord led. As I went to my knees, the fatigue rolled over me. I remember praying silently, "Lord, if

you don't energize me, I'll never make it. Please strengthen me
to enter into this prayer meeting." God definitely answered.
Several hours later, after a glorious time of meeting with the
Lord—and I mean glorious—we finished somewhere in the
early hours of the New Year. I did not want to stop. It was such
a precious time.

Asking

The second key word in the condition of symphonized
prayer is *ask*. The agreement is expressed through that which is
asked. The condition is "agreed asking," which is symphonized
prayer. The word *ask* involves several implications.

Real Prayer Is a Matter of Asking

In Elizabethan English the terms *pray* and *ask* were used
interchangeably. "I pray you" meant "I ask you." Therefore
real prayer is a petition. It is a matter of asking. Other matters,
such as thanksgiving, confession, and praise, may be included
under the broad umbrella of prayer, but specifically prayer is
asking.

Real Prayer Is a Petition to God

Since Jesus refers in the last phrase of verse 19 to His *Father*
as the one who answers the prayer, obviously the request
is directed to God. In corporate prayer meetings there is a
danger of using the prayer time as an opportunity to make
"announcements." Preachers may have more of a tendency to
fall into this. "Announcements" of other issues in the form of
prayer hinder real prayer. Real prayer is a petition to God—an
actual request—not an "announcement" to the group.

A corporate prayer meeting is not a time to display one's knowledge. John R. Rice once asked a preacher to pray in a meeting. As he prayed, the man quoted a multitude of verses. This is different than pleading a promise before the Throne. After the man finished, Rice said, "I noticed you quoted a lot verses. Do you think that God does not know those verses?" The preacher replied, "I didn't quote those verses for God's sake, but for the congregation's sake." Rice said, "That's the problem. You weren't praying to God!"

A corporate prayer meeting is not a time to instruct. How many times do prayers to God turn into instructions to man? As soon as one's prayer turns into instruction, he is no longer praying because God does not need to be instructed. Obviously, there is a time for the teaching and preaching of God's Word, but true prayer is a petition to God. Robert Murray McCheyne of Scotland's 1839 revival warned about this. He pointed out that when one prays in the flesh, another may be tempted to correct him in his prayer. McCheyne warned of pride and condescension entering in and the whole meeting getting off course. How much better it would be to follow the practice of John "Praying" Hyde. If others got off course, he simply stepped in and led the meeting back to the Throne—and he knew how to do it.

Real Prayer Is an Expression of Dependence

Another implication of *ask* is that real prayer is an expression of faith. The one being prayed to is the one being depended on. Real prayer is God-dependence. In fact, prayer is one of the major expressions of dependence on God. In a symphony of prayer, the faith of one will stir another to faith.

This is one of the blessings of real corporate prayer as already noted. Together there is a corporate trusting of God to work.

THE PROMISE OF SUPERNATURAL INTERVENTION

Jesus follows the condition in verse 19 with a tremendous promise: "it shall be done for them of my Father which is in heaven." Observe the phrase *it shall be done.* The next verse will explain why. But the point of this phrase is that the answer to this kind of praying is receiving. *It* (that which is asked) *shall be done.* That is what Jesus said.

Some have the idea that whatever happens is the answer to one's prayer. However, that concept without qualification can lead to fatalism. While it is true that when someone prays rightly, whatever happens is the answer. Yet when someone prays rightly, he receives that for which he asked. Contrariwise, it is possible to go through the motions of prayer in unbelief. In that case, whatever happens is not the answer. Many do not pray rightly and that is why they do not receive that for which they pray. But there is a right praying and in that case—*it shall be done.*

Some claim that they are trusting that God is working when in reality they have entered into a passivity regarding prayer. Before one can trust that God is working, he must first trust God to work. Then he can trust that God is working.

Faith is the missing ingredient in many prayers. For many, prayer is not much more than a religious duty. People go through the motions of prayer because they are supposed to, but there is not a sense of accessing the promises of God. Obviously, prayer does not change God because God is unchangeable. Also, prayer can change the one praying if he is truly seeking God's face. But real prayer changes things—things that otherwise would not have been changed if the prayer had not been prayed. It is possible to "have not, because ye ask not" (James 4:2). It is possible to limit the Holy One of Israel through unbelief (Ps. 78:41). But Spirit-led, Word-based, believing prayer opens the way for God's will to be done on earth as it is in heaven.

Jesus said it and meant it: *it shall be done.* The answer to the kind of prayer Jesus here describes is receiving that for which one has prayed. It is supernatural intervention.

THE REASON OF SPIRITUAL UNION

In verse 20 Jesus gives the reason that symphonized prayer accesses supernatural intervention: "For where two or three are gathered together in my name." The key phrase is *in my name.* In fact, the key to the whole Christian life is "in Christ." The New Testament is peppered with phrases such as *in Christ, in Him,* or *in my name.* These phrases occur nearly 250 times. To attempt to live the Christian life apart from a conscious dependence on life *in Christ* is to fall short of God's glory.

To have the fullest significance, prayer must be offered in conscious dependence on one's spiritual union with Christ. The believer is in Christ and Christ is in the believer. When this dynamic is realized by faith, one can move from the futility of praying in the flesh to the effectiveness of praying in the Spirit.

In light of this spiritual union consider two key realizations.

The Believer in Christ

The first realization involves the position of the believer: "you in Christ." When someone is born again, the Spirit places him in Christ (I Cor. 12:13). Every believer is *in Christ*. Christ sits at the Throne. Therefore every believer is in Christ at the Throne. Would not this realization change one's praying? At the Throne every believer is in the presence of God. "Let us therefore come boldly unto the throne of grace, that we may obtain mercy, and find grace to help in time of need" (Heb. 4:16).

In Christ every believer is privileged to pray "in my name." Praying in Christ's name has to do with authority. A child may have difficulty in getting his siblings to respond to his urgings to come to the supper table until he says, "Dad said!" Likewise, the name of Jesus carries authority. When a believer unites with the will of Christ, he may pray in Jesus' name— the authority of the enthroned Son of God.

Christ in the Believer

The second realization involves the partner of the believer: "Christ in you." When someone is born again, Christ places His Spirit into him (I Cor. 6:19). Therefore a believer must depend on his spiritual partner. Praying in Christ's name involves dependence on the Holy Spirit's leadership for what to pray and His enablement to pray it. When one truly trusts the Spirit as to what to pray, he will ask for greater things than he would have otherwise asked; therefore he will need the Spirit's enablement to pray it.

This is "praying in the Holy Ghost" (Jude 20). This is "praying always with all prayer and supplication in the Spirit" (Eph. 6:18). This is the Spirit's making "intercession for [through] us with groanings which cannot be uttered . . . according to the will of God" because "we know not what we should pray for as we ought" (Rom. 8:26–27).

Depend on the Spirit for Leadership in Prayer

Once while in a revival meeting with Charlie Kittrell (who was consumed with letting God be glorified through definite answers to prayer), he phoned me. He said that so-and-so kept coming to mind. He concluded that God wanted him to pray for so-and-so, and he phoned me to ask if I would pray as well. Then it occurred to me, "This is how the Spirit leads."

The Spirit is the Convincer (John 16:8), which of course affects the mind. He bears witness with the believer's spirit (Rom. 8:16), but He works through "the spirit of your mind" (Eph. 4:23). In other words, the Holy Spirit does not bypass one's faculties; He works through them. The Spirit leads by bringing issues to one's mind and then burdening one's spirit. I learned through this incident to be sensitive to that which keeps coming to mind with burden in the spirit as leadership from the Holy Spirit.

Depend on the Spirit for Enablement to Pray

Jonathan Goforth witnessed a great revival in Manchuria in 1908. He tells the story in his book *By My Spirit*. On one occasion while in the midst of nightly prayer meetings accompanied by life and blessing from the Lord, he noticed that whenever a certain man prayed, the meeting died. With caution he observed the same "killing of the meeting" over the next several nights whenever this certain man prayed. Finally, one night when this occurred, Goforth said, "Sir, please sit down. You are praying in the flesh." Afterwards the man thanked Goforth and admitted he was just praying because he saw all that was going on and he wanted to act like he was a part of it. Praying in the flesh is deadening to real prayer.

During a course on prayer taught by Charlie Kittrell at Baptist College of Ministry, a student asked, "Pastor Kittrell, does God ever say 'No' to you?" Pastor Kittrell looked over to his wife and asked, "Honey, does God ever say 'No' to us?" Then turning back to the student he said, "When you pray in the Spirit, God always says 'Yes!'" What a great truth! The Holy Spirit will not lead you to pray for that which He will not answer. This is why Jesus could say *it shall be done.* Although it may take time to discern the will of the Lord on a specific matter, once His will is known, believers can "ask" and expect "it shall be done."

Since the Holy Spirit is the conductor of a symphony of prayer, believers must obey the Spirit's leadership and depend on the Spirit's enablement. When the Spirit leads someone to pray, he must pray. To not do so would be to quench the Spirit. On the other hand, to pray when the Spirit has not led is to pray in the flesh. It is vital to obey the Holy Spirit. In fact, in a real symphony of prayer the Spirit may occasionally lead someone to sing, in which case all the others present would join. When the Spirit is leading and enabling, the harmony of heart is glorious.

In his book entitled *The Ministry of the Spirit*, A. J. Gordon addresses the topic of corporate prayer in his chapter entitled "The Administration of the Spirit."

The universal priesthood of believers, which the Scriptures so plainly teach, constitutes the ground for common intercession, for "the praying one for another" that is the distinctive feature of the Spirit's administration. The prayer meeting, therefore, in which the whole body of believers participates probably comes nearer the pattern of primitive Christian worship than any other service which we hold. To apply our principle here, then, what method is found most satisfactory? Shall the service be arranged before-hand, this one selected to pray, and that one to exhort; and during the progress of worship, shall such a one be called up to lead the devotions, and such a one to follow? After many years of experience, one can bear emphatic testimony to the value of another way—that of magnifying the office of the Holy Spirit as the leader of the service, and of so withholding the pressure of human hands in the assembly that the Spirit shall have the utmost freedom to move this one to pray and that one to witness, this one to sing and that one "to say amen at our giving of thanks," according to His own sovereign will. Here we speak not theoretically but experientially. The fervor and spirituality and sweet naturalness of the latter method has been demonstrated beyond a doubt. Our place is to honor the Holy Spirit as Master of our meetings; to study much the secret of surrender to Him; to cultivate a quick ear for hearing His inward voice and a ready tongue for speaking His audible witness; to submissively keep silent when He forbids as well as to speak when He commands, and we shall learn how much better is God's way of conducting the worship of His house than man's way.[2]

When God's people obey Christ's instructions for corporate prayer, they find that they actually meet with God. For Jesus said, "There am I in the midst of them."

A true symphony of prayer is an appointment with God. Therefore attending a Spirit-led corporate prayer meeting honors the presence of Jesus.

It used to be that I recoiled at the announcement of a corporate prayer meeting. Lifeless prayer meetings are deadening. Who wants to just go through ritualistic motions? But God changed my attitude in the summer of 2000 when the Spirit of revival swept through a church in Ireland that was pastored by David O'Gorman. Night after night in after-meetings (meetings following up the preaching meetings), God powerfully met with us. Before this, fifteen minutes of prayer often seemed to me like two hours. But in these prayer meetings two hours seemed like fifteen minutes. What a blessed difference!

The Spirit of revival swept through another meeting six months later with several Irish missionaries. In the midst of God manifesting His reviving presence, one preacher prayed with tears, "Lord, this is the closest thing to a Spirit-led prayer meeting I've ever been in!" Praise the Lord it was a Spirit-led prayer meeting—a true symphony of prayer!

THE INFLOW/OUTFLOW EXPERIMENT

Revival is a restoration to spiritual life. On the individual level this means that one begins to access the eternal life received at the new birth as the abundant life. It is accessing the indwelling life of Christ as the animating power to one's personality. It is walking by faith and therefore growing in grace. It is God-dependence accessing Spirit-enablement one step at a time. It is "I live; yet not I, but Christ" by "faith." It is life again!

Jesus is *the Life* of "life again." He delights in manifesting Himself in and through those who seek Him. *The Inflow/Outflow Experiment* simply applies the principles of seeking God. Just as an experiment in a school setting is not to see if something is so but to demonstrate that it is, so likewise the concept behind this "experiment" is an opportunity to allow God to demonstrate His life in and through you.

Outflow with no inflow is empty and pictures the attempt to serve God in the strength of the flesh instead of the power of the Spirit. Inflow with no outflow stagnates and pictures the deception of a life of faith without steps of faith. But an even inflow and outflow through a clean channel is full and flowing, picturing the Spirit-filled life for holiness and service.

INSTRUCTIONS

The Inflow/Outflow Experiment applies basic principles for the inflow of the Spirit's working *in* a believer's life and the outflow of the Spirit's working *through* a believer's life.

Inflow

The basic principles for *Inflow* are as follows (allow a minimum of thirty minutes for this time).

Read and meditate on a portion of God's Word. Ask the Holy Spirit to open your understanding and trust Him to reveal to you the realities of truth connected to the words of God. As you look unto Jesus, the living Word, the Holy Spirit will author faith in your heart by convincing you of the facts and promises that God intends for you to trust. Facts are in the present tense and represent present realities. Promises are in the future tense and represent potentialities. Both must be accessed by faith and may be as the Spirit of God convinces you of His Word and therefore His will.

Write down the insights that the Holy Spirit illumines to your heart.

Pray. Thank the Holy Spirit for speaking to you and revealing Christ. Confess any sin that the Spirit may convict you of and claim the cleansing power of the blood of Jesus. Then dare to face the facts (realities) of God's provision that the Spirit illumines to your heart and claim them as your present experience. Take them by faith that you may act upon them. Also dare to face the promises (potentialities) of God's provision that the Spirit illumines to your heart and obtain them as your expected experience. Ask for the Spirit's ministry to operate according to the promises. Ask for the leadership and enablement of the Spirit in the matter of witnessing to the lost. Take God's provision by faith that you may act in partnership with the Spirit.

As you "take" and "act" regarding the provision of God's facts (realities) and as you "ask," "take," and "act" regarding the provision of God's promises (potentialities), you are exercising faith through these simple steps. The Spirit will then finish your faith by enabling you according to the words of God.

Outflow

The basic principles for *Outflow* are as follows.

Implement the faith-filled steps of obedience that pertain to holiness in your life, trusting the Holy Spirit to enable you with the holy life of Christ. Trust to obey.

Testify to family members and others what God is doing for your soul.

Declare the gospel of Jesus Christ to someone in a definite way. Trust to obey the Holy Spirit's leadership as to who to give a gospel tract and who to engage in conversation. Find your divine appointment.

JOURNAL

The following daily journal masters on the next two pages may be copied and used to record the results of your inflow/ outflow experiment for thirty days. Ideally, you should try to meet once a week with others who are also applying this experiment and discuss the results together. Why not pray right now and ask the Lord for His guidance and blessing as you seek Him to demonstrate Himself through this experiment.

THE INFLOW/OUTFLOW JOURNAL

▶ *Inflow* *of the Holy Spirit*

Day: _____   Date: _____

You may want to review the *Inflow* instructions.

Read and meditate on a portion of God's Word, trusting the Holy Spirit for illumination.

Passage: _____

_____

Write down the insights that the Holy Spirit illumines to your heart.

_____
_____
_____
_____
_____
_____
_____
_____
_____
_____
_____
_____
_____
_____
_____
_____

Pray, remembering to ask for the ministry of the Holy Spirit and taking the provision by faith.

▶ *Outflow* of the Holy Spirit

You may want to review the *Outflow* instructions.

Implement any steps of obedience by trusting to obey.
Examples: _____

_____

_____

_____

_____

_____

_____

_____

_____

Testify to family members and others what God is doing for your soul.
Who you testified to: _____

_____

_____

_____

_____

_____

Declare the gospel of Jesus Christ in a definite way, trusting the Holy Spirit to lead you into divine appointments.
Divine appointments: _____

_____

_____

_____

Endnotes

CHAPTER ONE:

1 "As a verb, this root appears in three stems in Hebrew. The Qal conveys the basic meaning 'to live or have life,' whereas the two derived stems overlap in their meaning of 'giving or restoring life.'" R. Laird Harris, Gleason L. Archer, Jr., and Bruce K. Walke, *Theological Word Book of the Old Testament, Vol. I* (Chicago: Moody Press, 1981), 279–80. See also Francis Brown, S.R. Drivers, and Charles A. Briggs, *The New Brown-Driver-Briggs-Gesenius Hebrew and English Lexicon* (Peabody, MA: Hendrickson Publishers, Inc. 1979), 310–11.

2 Joseph Henry Thayer, *A Greek-English Lexicon of the New Testament* (Grand Rapids: Baker Book House, 1977), 37.

3 William F. Arndt and F. Wilbur Gingrich, *A Greek-English Lexicon of the New Testament* (Chicago: The University of Chicago Press, 1979), 53.

4 Noah Webster, *American Dictionary of the English Language.* 1828 ed. http://1828.mshaffer.com/d/search/word, revive, (Internet, accessed 12 July 2007).

5 Ibid.

6 Ibid.

7 Ruth Paxson, *The Wealth, Walk, and Warfare of the Christian* (New York: Fleming H. Revell Company, 1939), 156.

8 Rick Flanders's excellent little book entitled *Back to Normal* expands this thought in a truly helpful way (Vasser, MI: Revival Ministries, n.d.), 1–67.

9   John Greenfield, *When the Spirit Came* (Minneapolis: Bethany Fellowship, Inc., 1967), 1-94.

10   J. Edwin Orr, *The Fervent Prayer: The Worldwide Impact of the Great Awakening of 1858* (Chicago: Moody Press, 1974), 11.

11   J. Edwin Orr, *The Flaming Tongue: The Impact of Early 20th Century Revivals* (Chicago: Moody Press, 1975), 1–200.

12   Orr, *The Fervent Prayer*, vii.

CHAPTER TWO:

1   Jonathan Goforth, *By My Spirit* (Nappanee, IN: Evangel Publishing House, n.d.), 54.

2   R. Laird Harris, Gleason L. Archer, Jr., and Bruce K. Waltke, *Theological Workbook of the Old Testament, Vol. 2* (Chicago: Moody Press, 1980), 901.

3   Francis Brown, S. R. Driver, and Charles A. Briggs, *The New Brown-Driver-Briggs-Gesenius Hebrew and English Lexicon* (Peabody, MA: Hendrickson Publishers, Inc., 1979), 990.

4   William F. Arndt and F. Wilbur Gingrich, *A Greek-English Lexicon of the New Testament and Other Early Christian Literature*, 2d ed. rev. F. Wilbur Gingrich and Fredrick W. Danker (Chicago: University of Chicago Press, 1979), 793.

5   Brown, Driver, and Briggs, 194.

6   Ibid., 1050.

7   Harris, Archer, and Waltke, 445.

8   Nancy Leigh DeMoss, *Brokenness: The Heart God Revives* (Chicago: Moody Press, 2002), 51.

9   Ibid., 50.

10   Ibid., 52–54.

11   Fritz Rienecker and Cleon L. Rogers, Jr., *A Linguistic Key to the Greek New Testament* (Grand Rapids: Regency Reference Library, 1980), 786.

12   Goforth, 85–86.

13   Stanley C. Griffin, *A Forgotten Revival* (Great Britain: Day One Publications, 2000), 16–18.

14   Roy Hession, *The Calvary Road* (Fort Washington, PA: Christian Literature Crusade Publications, 2000), 126.

15   I. R. Govan, *The Spirit of Revival* (Edinburgh: The Faith Mission, 1938, 4th ed. 1978), 25.

16   Ibid., 23, 25.

17   Ibid., 21.

CHAPTER THREE:
1   Andrew A. Woolsey, *Channel of Revival: A Biography of Duncan Campbell* (Edinburgh: The Faith Mission, reprint 1982), 139–41.

2   Duncan Campbell, *The Nature of a God-Sent Revival* (Vinton, VA: Christ Life Publications, reprint n.d.), 9.

3   Duncan Campbell, *The Lewis Awakening* in *Heritage of Revival* by Colin N. Peckham (Edinburgh: The Faith Mission, 1986), 174–75.

4   For further study on the biblical phraseology of the outpouring of the Spirit in both the Old and the New Testaments, see John R. VanGelderen, Chapter 12: "The Age of Pentecost" in *The Wind of the Spirit in Personal and Corporate Revival* (Menomonee Falls, WI: Preach the Word Ministries, Inc., 2003), 161–77.

5   R. B. Jones, *Rent Heavens* (Asheville, NC: Revival Literature, reprint, n.d.), 42.

6   Woolsey, 121.

7   Arnold Dallimore, *George Whitefield,* Vol. II (Carlisle, PA: Banner of Truth, reprint, n.d.), 129.

8   David Matthews, *I Saw the Welsh Revival* (Asheville, NC: Revival Literature, 2004), 46.

9   Jones, 40–41.

10   G. Campbell Morgan, "The Revival: Its Source and Power" in *Revival* magazine, January–April 2005 (Menomonee Falls, WI: Preach the Word Ministries, Inc., 2005), 5.

11   Woolsey, 71–72.

12   Ibid., 117–18.

13   Jones, 41–42.

14   Dallimore, 129.

15   Ian Paisley, *The "Fifty-Nine" Revival* (Belfast: Martyrs Memorial Free Presbyterian Church, 1958, reprint 1987), 37.

16   Woolsey, 51.

17   J. Edwin Orr, *The Fervent Prayer: The Worldwide Impact of the Great Awakening of 1858* (Chicago: Moody Press, 1974), 11.

18   J. Edwin Orr, *The Flaming Tongue: The Impact of Early 20th Century Revivals* (Chicago: Moody Press, 1975), 186.

19   Michael Redick, "The Wind of Revival in the Chin Hills," in *Revival* magazine, January–April 2006 (Menomonee Falls, WI: Preach the Word Ministries, Inc., 2006), 3–4.

20   Michael Redick, "A Passionate Plea for Revival," in *Revival* magazine, May–August 2006 (Menomonee Falls, WI: Preach the Word Ministries, Inc., 2006), 11.

21   Redick, "The Wind of Revival in the Chin Hills," 4.

22   Jessie Penn-Lewis, *The Awakening in Wales* (Fort Washington, PA: Christian Literature Crusade Publications, 2002 reprint), 45–46.

CHAPTER FOUR:
1   R. Laird Harris, Gleason L. Archer, Jr., and Bruce K. Waltke, *Theological Wordbook of the Old Testament* (Chicago: Moody Press, 1980), 126.

2   Ibid., 198.

3   All 70 occurrences are referenced in this chapter. There are other contexts of seeking or inquiring after God, but clearly not with a whole heart. In these contexts of half-hearted seeking, there is no finding.

4   Walter C. Kaiser, *Quest for Renewal* (Chicago: Moody Press, 1986), 13–14.3

5   J. Edwin Orr, *The Flaming Tongue: The Impact of Early 20th Century Revivals* (Chicago: Moody Press, 1975), 61.

6   Iain Murray, *J. Edward: A New Biography* (Edinburgh: The Banner of Truth Trust, 1987, reprint 2000), 169.

7   Ibid., 168.

8   Orr, 200.

9   Christo von Staden, "The Story of the Great Revival of 1860 in Worcester" and "The 1860 Revival Shook the Entire Native Countryside," *Worcester Standard* (May, 2001).

4   For a further study on the access of faith based on John 14:12, see John R. Van Gelderen, Chapter 13: "From Greater Words to Greater Works" in *The Wind of the Spirit in Personal and Corporate Revival* (Menomonee Falls, WI: Preach the Word Ministries, Inc., 2003), 181–92.

5   For an expansion of this concept, see Appendix A: "A Symphony of Prayer."

6   J. Edwin Orr, *The Eager Feet: Evangelical Awakenings, 1790–1830* (Chicago: Moody Press, 1975), 1–248.

7   For a biblical background and explanation of the Solemn Assembly, see Richard Owen Roberts, *The Solemn Assembly* (Wheaton: International Awakening Press, 1989), 1–15.

8   Ian Paisley, *The "Fifty-Nine" Revival* (Belfast: Martyrs Memorial Free Presbyterian Church, 1958, reprint 1987), 17.

CHAPTER FIVE:
1   Stewart Custer, *Witness to Christ: A Commentary on Acts* (Greenville, SC: Bob Jones University Press, 2000), xix.

2   Evan Hopkins quoted in Alexander Smellie, *Evan Henry Hopkins: A Memoir* (London: Marshall Brothers Limited, 1920), 71.

3   Jonathan Goforth, *By My Spirit* (Nappanee, IN: Evangel Publishing House, n.d.) 19–21.

4   Ibid., 22–23.

5   Ibid., 1–138.

CHAPTER SIX:
1   In Luke 15, Jesus narrates the parable of "The Lost Sheep," "The Lost Coin," and "The Prodigal Son." While it is true that all three stories are referred to as "this parable" (15:3), yet there is a difference of emphasis in the first two stories from that of the third. The emphasis of "The Lost Sheep" and "The Lost Coin" is salvation, but the emphasis of "The Prodigal Son" is revival for the following reasons: (1) The first two stories regard a "sinner," but the third story regards a "son." (2) The summation of the first two stories speak of joy in heaven "over one sinner that repenteth" (15:7, 10), but the summary of the third story is of a son being "alive again." (3) The third story describes a son as having the inheritance of the father in the phrase "all that I have is thine" (15:31). This is not true of lost sinners. (4) The first two stories emphasize the sinner being sought, but the third story emphasizes the son seeking.

Although the emphasis varies between salvation and revival, revival is like getting saved and may be described as being made "alive again" or being "found" (15:24, 32).

2   Andrew A. Woolsey, *Channel of Revival: A Biography of Duncan Campbell* (Edinburgh: The Faith Mission, reprint 1982), 118.

3   Ibid., 114.

4   Ibid., 114–15.

5   J. Edwin Orr, *The Eager Feet: Evangelical Awakenings, 1790–1830* (Chicago: Moody Press, 1975), 1–248.

6   Roy Hession, *The Calvary Road* (Fort Washington, PA: Christian Literature Crusade Publications, 2000), 1–134 and *We Would See Jesus* (Fort Washington, PA: Christian Literature Crusade Publications, 2005), 1–154.

7   For more information in this regard, see Chapter 7: "Perils of the Victorious Life" in Charles Trumbull, *Victory in Christ* (Fort Washington PA: Christian Literature Crusade Publications, 1979, reprint 2007) and Jessie Penn-Lewis with Evan Roberts, *War on the Saints* (New York: Thomas E. Lowe, Ltd., reprint 1991).

8   R. A. Torrey, *How to Pray* (Old Tappan, NJ: Fleming H. Revell Company, 1900 reprint 1976) 34–35.

9   Jonathan Edwards, "The Distinguishing Marks of a Work of God" in *Jonathan Edwards on Revival* (Edinburgh: The Banner of Truth Trust, 1984) 75–147.

10   Marie Monsen, *The Awakening: Revival in China, A Work of the Holy Spirit* (Runnells, IA: Burning Heart Publications, 1959 © Gry Forlag, 1961 © China Inland Mission reprint 2007) 1–113.

11   Jessie Penn-Lewis, *The Awakening on Wales* (Fort Washington, PA: Christian Literature Crusade Publications, 1993 reprint 2002), 7.

Selected Bibliography

Campbell, Duncan. *The Lewis Awakening*. In *Heritage of Revival* by Colin N. Peckham. Edinburgh: The Faith Mission, 1986.

———. *The Nature of a God-Sent Revival*. Vinton, VA: Christ Life Publications, n.d.

Dallimore, Arnold. *George Whitefield*. Carlisle, PA: The Banner of Truth Trust, n.d.

DeMoss, Nancy Leigh. *Brokenness: The Heart God Revives*. Chicago: Moody Press, 2002.

Edwards, Jonathan. "The Distinguishing Marks of a Work of God." In *Jonathan Edwards on Revival*. Edinburgh: The Banner of Truth Trust, 1984.

Flanders, Rick. *Back to Normal*. Vasser, MI: Revival Ministries, n.d.

Goforth, Jonathan. *By My Spirit*. Nappanee, IN: Evangel Publishing House, n.d.

Gordon, A. J. *The Ministry of the Holy Spirit*. Minneapolis: Bethany House Publishers, 1985.

Govan, I. R. *The Spirit of Revival*. Edinburgh: The Faith Mission, 1978.

Greenfield, John. *When the Spirit Came*. Minneapolis: Bethany Fellowship, Inc., 1967.

Griffin, Stanley C. *A Forgotten Revival*. Great Britain: Day One Publications, 2000.

Hession, Roy. *The Calvary Road*. Fort Washington, PA: Christian Literature Crusade Publications, 2000.

———. *We Would See Jesus*. Fort Washington, PA: Christian Literature Crusade Publications, 2005.

Jones, R. B. *Rent Heavens*. Asheville, NC: Revival Literature, n.d.

Kaiser, Walter C. *Quest for Revival*. Chicago: Moody Press, 1986.

Matthews, David. *I Saw the Welsh Revival*. Asheville, NC: Revival Literature, 2004.

Monsen, Marie. *The Awakening: Revival in China, A Work of the Holy Spirit*. Runnells, IA: Burning Heart Publications, 2007.

Morgan, G. Campbell. "The Revival: Its Source and Power." *Revival* magazine, January-April 2005. Menomonee Falls, WI: Preach the Word Ministries. Inc., 2005.

Orr, J. Edwin. *The Eager Feet: Evangelical Awakenings, 1790-1830*. Chicago, Moody Press, 1975.

———. *The Fervent Prayer: The Worldwide Impact of the Great Awakening of 1858*. Chicago: Moody Press, 1974.

———. *The Flaming Tongue: The Impact of the Early 20th Century Revivals*. Chicago: Moody Press, 1975.

Paisley, Ian. *The "Fifty Nine" Revival*. Belfast: Martyrs Memorial Free Presbyterian Church, 1987.

Paxson, Ruth. *The Wealth, Walk, and Warfare of the Christian*. New York: Fleming H. Revell Company, 1939.

Penn-Lewis, Jessie. *The Awakening in Wales*. Fort Washington, PA: Christian Literature Crusade Publications, 2002.

Penn-Lewis, Jessie, and Evan Roberts. *War on the Saints*. New York: Thomas E. Lowe, Ltd., 1991.

Redick, Michael. "A Passionate Plea for Revival." *Revival* magazine, May-August 2006. Menomonee Falls, WI: Preach the Word Ministries, Inc., 2006.

———. "The Wind of Revival in the Chin Hills." *Revival* magazine, January-April 2006. Menomonee Falls, WI: Preach the Word Ministries, Inc., 2006.

Smellie, Alexander. *Evan Henry Hopkins: A Memoir.* London: Marshall Brothers Limited, 1920.

Torrey, R. A. *How to Pray.* Old Tappan, NJ: Fleming H. Revell Company, 1976.

Trumbull, Charles. *Victory in Christ.* Fort Washington, PA: Christian Literature Crusade Publications, 2007.

Woolsey, Andrew A. *Channel of Revival: A Biography of Duncan Campbell.* Edinburgh: The Faith Mission, 1982.

$3.00

$15.00

35181966R10106

Made in the USA
Middletown, DE
23 September 2016